Donna Howell, Allie Henson & Nita Horn

MisFits

LEARNING FROM OUR INNER OUTCAST AND HOW
IT CAN EMPOWER US TO FIND OUR DESTINY

DEFENDER

CRANE, MO

MISFITS: LEARNING FROM OUR INNER OUTCAST AND HOW IT
CAN EMPOWER US TO FIND OUR DESTINY
by Donna Howell, Allie Henson, Nita Horn

Simply His, a division of Defender Publishing
Crane, MO 65633
© 2021 Thomas Horn

ISBN: 9781948014540

A CIP catalog record of this book is available from the Library of Congress.

Cover design by Jeffrey Mardis.

All Scripture quoted is from the King James Version unless otherwise noted.

To God and family:
our anchors through every storm.

~

And to Nancy, whose candid conversation
inspired much of this book.

Contents

Part 1

We're All Misfits Here

The world is made up of unique and eccentric people—those who only fit in when they find the courage to step out and find their place. The choice remains for each of us to make as to whether we will do so or remain isolated. Are we no different from the toys that occupy an island far from their peers in that we will allow ourselves to live out the same fate, missing all that our lives could be? Or will we find the courage to emerge and live life to the fullest, finding our place within the world, our communities, and even in the Body of Christ?

1

I Am the Bearded Lady

By Donna Howell

For children, few things can compare to the magic of the holidays. The scent of baking cookies, the sound of wrapping paper rustling, the brush of chilly, wintry air on your face, or the sound of a crackling fire below a row of hanging stockings are all thoughts that may come to mind at the mention of "Christmas." Of course, for those of us who have taken Jesus as personal Lord and Savior, there is a deeper element to Christmas—that which celebrates the greatest gift that mankind has ever been given—the gift of salvation.

It would seem that, regardless of how the world changes throughout the rest of the year, the timeless essence of this holiday remains pristine and unscathed by the goings-on of the world. The precious traditions of this cherished day remain memorialized in our thoughts forever—and are quickly called back at the mere manifestation of a song, a taste, or even a scent. At just the right mental cue, it can be as though we're youngsters again, enjoying time with those we spent cherished days with in our early years.

And then, there are icons that recall nearly everyone to a time of their youth: Christmas carols, classic holiday movies, cartoons, poems, and more. These, because of their connections to these special days, often adopt a special place in our hearts, offering the ability to carry us backward in time, allowing us the chance to revisit days long gone. For me, one of the most compelling of these is the 1964 Rankin & Bass production *Rudolph the Red-Nosed Reindeer*. As a child, I watched and rewatched this movie, absorbed its fantastical scenes, and sang along with every tune. Even now, this film has the power to take me back to childhood: nights curled up on a blanket in our living room floor, trying not to fall asleep before the movie ended. (This was before we owned a VCR, meaning that the one night each year this flick was broadcast might be my only shot to see the movie until the next year.) I would laugh during the funny moments; sympathize with poor Rudolph, who just couldn't fit in because of his shiny nose; gasp in fear of the Abominable Snowman; and stare wide-eyed at the toy-laden abundance of the North Pole.

But in addition to all of that, most kids, like me, would also take in the Island of the Misfit Toys: that place where all the oddball or abnormal toys deemed unworthy to be Christmas presents were discarded. We wondered *why* such eccentricities as a squirt gun that shoots jelly instead of water was doomed to isolation for the duration of its days. Or, why a Jack-in-the-Box toy named Charlie—thus rendering him a Charlie-in-the-Box—was on these grounds, forever banished from the merriment of childhood play. Then, of course, there were other toys—like the dolly for Sue, the scooter for Jimmy, and others—who seemed to have no peculiarities whatsoever. Despite their lack of irregularity, they too, faced exile. Why?

We can quickly begin to see a parallel between the fate of these fictional playthings and that of many people who live, each day, in self-imposed isolation. The truth is that if each person who, like these toys, is a misfit, was to stay sequestered from the outside world, nobody would ever leave their front door. In actuality, we authors assert that the world is made up of unique and eccentric people—those who only fit in when they find the courage to step out and find their place. And, the choice remains for each of us to make as to whether we will do so or remain isolated. Are we no different from these items that occupy an island far from their peers in that we will allow ourselves to live out the same fate, missing all that our lives could be? Or will we find the courage to emerge and live life to the fullest, finding our place within the world, our communities, and even in the Body of Christ?

Each of the toys in this simple movie can teach us volumes about ourselves if we'll take the time to understand what we can glean from them. Before exploring this, however, I must deviate from the topic of this classic Christmas movie to explain how God revealed my identity in Him to me. He didn't do this through *Rudolph*, however, but through a more recent production.

A few years ago, I experienced one of the more amazing demonstrations of God's communication in my life. The clarity of His voice has only been *this* clear and incredible a few times in my entire walk with Him, and this lesson from our precious Lord had His sense of humor written all over it. I laughed, cried, clapped, and wiggled around in my seat. His message to me not only came repeatedly—*and* in the exact same framework of delivery—but it also came to me in "layers" of depth. In other words, each time I listened to what He was telling me, I found layers of meaning I hadn't caught before.

Knowing I needed to document what was happening at the time while my thoughts and feelings were fresh, I sat down at my computer one night and began typing. I worked on the piece, titled "Heroic Freaks," clickety-clacking away at the keyboard without stopping until it was all on the screen.

I had *no* idea if I would ever share this testimony with anyone, or if it would float around in my computer for years and only minister to me, myself, when I wanted to remember the season when God defined me in the sweetest and most comically memorable light...but it didn't matter. A Still Voice told me to record what happened, so I did...

Months later, I received a call from Thomas Horn, CEO of Defender Publishing and SkyWatch Television (as you might already know, he's also my dad). Like oh so many times prior, he had another book he wanted me to consider writing. This time it was "The Island of Misfit Toys," he said. "From *Rudolph*! All those toys that feel broken and useless, never being chosen by Santa to ride the sleigh to a child's home where they can fulfill a purpose. The symbolism of the lion on the island. The 'Charlie-in-the-box,' the squirt gun that only shoots peanut butter and jelly, the train with square wheels. It's all there! You know where I'm going with this, right?"

Of course I did. I knew from the word "misfits" where he was "going with this."

Why? How?

Because it was *my* testimony that my father was asking me to write. Funny thing? He didn't know it yet. He didn't have a clue. And even funnier? I had completely forgotten I had written that "Heroic Freaks" testimony piece. It had been wiped from my memory, and would remain so, until God wanted me to recall it.

After spending the next several months finishing up a few other major writing projects I had already been obligated to, I took time to scribble out what I thought would be a draft outline for this *Misfits* book. I had a decent grasp on what subjects and bullet points the book would bob around on in the middle, and I felt the end would flow from that nicely. But the very beginning—the opening thought of the whole manuscript that sets the pace for all else that will be said—*that* eluded me entirely. Every idea I had seemed desperate, so I decided to leave it open-ended and get started by compiling a few thoughts from the Apostle Paul's writings that I knew I would eventually tackle at some point.

Then, as if it had been planned from the beginning by some Source higher than myself, the beginning I couldn't plan out fell right into my lap...literally.

Part 1: We're All Misfits Here

My computer area at home is a pileup. I'm not gonna lie. I wish I could be like the briefcasey, high-heelsey, tight-bunned, "results on the desk by Monday" types you see on television and in movies where every pencil has its place and every paper is filed away properly, but, meh…I have my priorities (personal Bible study, kids, hubby, college, career, organic dietary living…full-time everything, all the time), so I'm not worried about papers on my desk being in their proper place all the time. Just a day or two after I had tried to iron out the *Misfits* outline, I was going through some old papers, digging for something unrelated that a college professor needed from me, and as I reached to sort the heap on top of my dinosauric HP Deskjet printer, an enormous glob of napkins with scribbled writing spewed out at me. I caught them with my knees, and after setting everything else down, picked them up to have a look. I immediately remembered all those nights in the darkness of the movie theater, wrestling with a pen and napkins to record my thoughts in the moment they occurred. It was from these notes that I had eventually put together the "Heroic Freaks" piece…

I was floored! There it was—the beginning of this book. That puzzling blip that the Holy Spirit had nudged me to write a year earlier was coming into play in a way that I couldn't have ever arranged. It couldn't have been clearer that the Lord had led me to write—and then to forget that I wrote—about one of the most amazing lessons on His voice that I would ever experience, just so I would find it at this precise moment.

I jumped to my Microsoft Windows "Type here to search" field and located the original reflection of that time in my life. Upon reading it, I was amazed at how many details of the original story I had forgotten since then. Sure enough, it was the *perfect* way to start this book, and it doesn't get more personal than this.

The following is my own "Freak" testimony, just as I wrote it in February of 2018…

Freak

It's almost ten o'clock at night as I write this. I arrived home only minutes ago from the movie theaters for the fifth time in a little over a week. Despite the late hour, my mind is once again wide awake, racing with this unexpected obsession of mine over—of all things—a modern musical film.

How silly—right?

The first time I saw *The Greatest Showman* starring Hugh Jackman as renowned entrepreneur Phineas T. Barnum of the historically celebrated Barnum & Bailey Circus, I was so weepy halfway through that I missed several portions of the movie simply trying to bring myself back to planet earth. So help me, I could not stop crying. And before it's assumed to be a habit of mine to frequent movie theaters for a good ol'-fashioned emotional meltdown, believe me when I say this had *never* happened before. Nor have I ever been so compulsively consumed by a movie that I had to see it five times in a row. At this very moment, I'm still desperately scouring my mind to try to find a couple free hours in the next few days so I can experience the film a sixth time. [Note: I eventually saw this movie eleven times before it left theaters. Each time was as powerful as the time before.]

Certainly, there are the obvious reasons to jump on the fanatical bandwagon affecting half the globe since [the December 2017] theatrical release—no nudity, gore, or profanity whatsoever, so it's a clean bit of entertainment for all ages; the cast has excellent chemistry; the score is fresh and stimulating; the choreography is deliciously crisp and precise; and, well, who doesn't love Hugh Jackman? But the real reason I was completely wrecked by this film had nothing to do with why the rest of the theater was sniffling and reaching for the travel-sized Kleenex pouches in the bottom of their handbags; it was because of what that Still, Small Voice whispered to me during several key scenes...

"You are the bearded lady."

Yes, I know. That's so far out of left field that it circles the moon. Bear with me…

From the opening credits, a weight hit the pit of my stomach. It's never happened before, but as God is my witness, before the plot even began to unfold, I had been pricked with a sense of "knowing" that I needed to pay very close attention. God had something to say to me. "Listen closely," I felt like He was whispering. "Watch this plot and remember."

I am not so naïve that I would assume P. T. Barnum's life was 100 percent accurately portrayed in this musical extravaganza, so I will not spend time trying to romanticize his actions in every scene. I do, however, want to take a quick moment to explain the backdrop of the story (*as portrayed in this movie, not necessarily in historical record*), so my own personal revelation will be better understood.

As a boy, P. T. Barnum's dreams are larger than life (as is told through the song "A Million Dreams"). After the death of his father leaves him homeless and hungry, young Barnum tries to steal some bread. He is chased down, thrown to the ground, and left to starve. In that moment, a hand reaches out and offers him an apple. Barnum looks up and sees that the hand belongs to a woman with a greatly disfigured face, but behind the deformity, there's a compassion—a depth of character and kindness that can only come from another tortured soul.

As an adult, Barnum channels his colorful dreams into a museum of "macabre wonders" (taxidermy animals and human wax sculptures) to provide his wife the life he promised her—but when the business fails to take off, his insightful little girls convince him that his collection of oddities involves too many stuffed exhibits, and he needs to bring life to the museum. His memories take him back to the apple offered by the unusual woman on the street, and he is hit with a sudden epiphany to fill his museum with living human spectacles. It is then that we observe his first recruit: Charles Stratton, a full-grown, yet tiny, dwarf—who later became known (in the movie and in real life) as "General Tom

Thumb" as a result of his costume and horse-riding act. This conversation represents a turning point in the plot development:

BARNUM: I'm putting together a show, and I need a star.

STRATTON: [Hesitating...] You want people to laugh at me.

BARNUM: Well, they're laughing, anyway, kid, so you may as well get paid.

[Stratton shuts the door in Barnum's face, and Barnum realizes he has to approach this thing differently. He pauses, gets down on his knees to Stratton's level, and speaks through the door knob.]

BARNUM: I see a soldier—no, a *general*—riding across the stage with a sword and a gun, and the most beautiful uniform ever made. People will come from all over the world, and when they see him, they won't laugh. [Stratton opens the door.] They'll *salute.*[1]

At this point in the film, the audience is given a peek into the genius behind Barnum's plan. On one hand, he will draw in crowds who are mesmerized by sensational sideshow curiosities—those who will pay any price to see General Tom Thumb trotting past the Irish Giant as he dances with the ghostly albino woman who's waving to Jo-Jo the Dog-Faced Boy as he howls across the stage to the 750-pound "World's Heaviest Man." Far more important to the viewing audience of today, however, is the underlying concept that Barnum is rescuing these poor souls—these pitiful people whom society openly calls "freaks"—from a life of shame and hiding, just as he had been rescued by the unusual apple-lady as a boy. Because of Barnum, these scorned men and women will now have a place to call home, a new family of fellow oddities who will love beyond an exterior, and a new purpose.

The parallel that the Lord wanted me to see was forming already, and for one brief moment, I thought that was all He wanted me to absorb. It wasn't even the tip of the iceberg, but what I had gained so far was enough material for fifty books:

The Circus: Under no normal, natural circumstances would a gathering of societal throwaways in the 1800s be even so much as considered equal, let alone celebrated, for their uniqueness—but in the Barnum ring, the "freaks" become the "heroes."

The Church: Under no normal, natural circumstances would a gathering of shattered people with weaknesses, baggage, past trauma, and pain be chosen as the central mouthpieces of something as grand as the salvation and redemption of the gospel—but in the true Church of Jesus Christ, the "broken" become the "beautiful."

People are drawn in by the Church's promise that their brokenness will not stop them from a calling higher than their own self, and that in this Body of believers, they will have a new family and a new home. God won't just use willing people "in spite of" their mistakes and past, He will use them "because of" their mistakes and past. It's due to the limitations and mistakes of our humanity that we can ever reach and affect the lives of others. It is only when we have something in common with those around us that we can make a connection, and then a difference. This pattern is how the Church began. Once again: Under no *normal, natural circumstances* would a Jew and a tax collector be seen together, but at Christ's table, the "enemies" become "brothers." A new family of oddities is formed, and no one is alone.

I hear You, Lord, I said in my thoughts as I watched Hugh Jackman shake hands with the dwarf to seal the deal. *Where the world sees a lump of useless clay, You see the finished vase.*

In case you haven't yet heard, that has been my ministry for several years straight now. I even wrote a book about it (*Radicals*). This message of pulling others out of their comfort bubbles and into the fullness of their ministerial potential has been my heartbeat. If that moment in the theater had been the end of the revelation the Lord wanted me to receive, it would have been plenty, simply because this Hugh Jackman/Barnum character had already provided me the five-point outline for a billion sermons that were already familiar and burning within me. I smiled and clapped, and then nonchalantly returned to my popcorn, not suspecting for a moment it would get any deeper. But that's when Barnum met *her*...

"Hey!" a man on the street says to Barnum as he was nailing up a want ad for human curiosities. "You lookin' for *freaks*? I know where you can find one of *them*."

"Really," Barnum says, intrigued.[2]

In the next scene, he follows a powerful singing voice to a woman who's hidden behind white sheets in a washroom. As she sees him approach, she immediately yet timidly asks him to leave. He counters with a comment of her astounding talent and whisks the sheets out of the way, revealing a heavyset woman with a full-grown beard. His eyes grow wide and he calls her "extraordinary."

Once again, a "freak" to the world is recognized by Barnum as "extraordinary." She has value, he says. She has purpose, he says. The world doesn't see it yet, he says, but soon, they will.[3]

Before another scripted word was delivered, that Still, Small Voice I have only recently begun to fully hear and recognize said, "You are the bearded lady."

Oh... I'm one of the freaks in this story, too? I asked the Lord silently.

"You're the biggest one."

Pause for a crucial clarification.

No, God does not go around calling people "freaks." There is nothing theologically sound about that. You have to understand the word in context to two contributing factors: 1) the film's use of the term (literal circus freaks), and 2) my own past use of the term...

Between God and myself, there has been a very personal meaning to that word for the last several years. I've even said it aloud during prayers...a lot! For example, here's one I've gone rounds with for five straight years:

God, why are You calling such a freak of nature to do Your work?! Nothing about me makes sense! I ask to be used, but then I hate what I'm asked to do. You ask me to be proud of my femininity and my womanly place, but I detest personally participating in the cosmetic routines of other women in my line of work. You ask me to be bold, and even empower me with boldness, and then when the microphone is placed in front of me, I shrink away for reasons even I don't comprehend. If I am really supposed to be a preacher, a teacher, and an author, then why am I so uncomfortable doing all of that? Why do I loathe so strongly the spotlight if that's where you've called me to stand? I *so* desire your will for me, but I also *so* desire to crawl into a cave and just be left anonymous. Obeying your orders is scary to me. Others would give anything to have the opportunities that I have, and I would give anything to trade places with them for their anonymity. You have given me the talent to do what I'm doing, and I want to be used, but I don't want to be used in the area of my talents. Ugh! Why do I have to be such a *freak*?

In my conversations with God, the word "freak" has slowly taken on new definitions. From the *Donna Howell Dictionary*:

freak (freek), *noun*: 1. A person who feels like a reject, but whom God calls to serve Him in surprising ways. 2. A person who asks to be used by God, asks for the strength needed to be used in the position He's called them into, and then, when He gives the individual precisely what he or she asked for, he or she then waveringly cowers into a corner and asks to be left alone.

This was the personal definition on my mind when Barnum confronts Lettie, the bearded lady, in the washroom. As if on cue, the very next words out of Lettie's mouth are, "Sir, please leave me alone."[4]
Whoa… Okay Lord, I'm listening.
I was already the bearded lady, Lettie, on several counts, but as the scenes played out on the screen in front of me, it quickly became unreal

how many parallels there were between us. One moment in my life was almost identical to one that Lettie's character was about to face.

I had been invited to preach at Jim Bakker's *The Prophets Speak* evening service show during the production's 56th Annual 4th of July Celebration in 2017. Jim's audience was getting to know me pretty quickly of late, as I had been on his programs several times in relation to the release of my *Radicals* book. At one point during one of the several filming sessions, I got inspired to look right into the camera and encourage people to believe in their calling and in their voice, and when I had finished saying what I had to say, the room erupted in the first of two standing ovations that I would receive that day. Needless to say, the impression that was left was a decent one, but it wasn't anything I had known to plan for. God had taken over—that much was obvious—and because it happened at the spur of the moment, I didn't have any time to get worked up about it in advance.

Independence Day at Jim's Morningside Church in Blue Eye, Missouri, is the biggest event of each year, and attendance is at record highs. They invited me to preach that Friday night, the last night, "to take us out with a bang!" Jim had said. I knew they all had elevated expectations because of the bar being set so high the day of the two standing ovations, so I was already nervous when I accepted the invitation. Then, the day before my scheduled sermon, Jim told me in front of a packed studio audience that he wanted me to "let loose, preach away, and drive it home!" The response from everyone told me that, yes, they were all expecting the "radical ovation Donna" that they had seen before, and I had no idea how to bring that to the stage again since it hadn't really been *me* who had brought it the first time. Prior to this moment, I had only spoken two times in my life, with both engagements in front of about ten people.

By this point, I was incredibly intimidated by the task before me. But the worst part was when I was getting hooked up to the sound system ten minutes before I was due on the platform. Let me explain…

First of all, I had left my sermon notes at the hotel, and there wasn't time to return for them, so I had to preach the entire word from memory. Of course, I had practiced that sermon probably five hundred times, so operating from memory wasn't the most incomprehensible idea—but still, you don't just go gallivanting off to preach without notes! That was messing with my head, big time, because if I drew a blank like I did frequently while I had been rehearsing at home—those hours I spent encouraging my daughter's stuffed animals to realize that they, too, were called for great things—then I would have nothing else to lean on…and that irrefutably meant freezing up at the famous church. Terrifying.

Second, I was physically very ill, faint, and exhausted. In fact, I was sicker that day than I had been in years due to a health condition that was becoming increasingly all-consuming. Any time I stood up, I would almost faint, and had to keep grabbing onto sturdy objects around me to keep from falling; my husband, James, was pumping me full of vitamins and telling the kids to give me space while the world swirled and spun around me the whole morning and afternoon; I couldn't keep a whole meal down, so the powders James was having me drink made me "vitamin sick" on top of how dreadful I already felt; and I hadn't slept at all the night before because, between an uncomfortable hotel bed and my nerves, tossing and turning was the only reality for me.

Third, though I had support from Jim and his audience, I had recently come under attack online for being a female teacher/preacher from the last *Jim Bakker Show* episode that aired, so the chances that another wave of people opposing me and making me the center of attention in all the wrong ways was a strong possibility. I loathed knowing that, by doing something God asked me to do, I was putting myself in a position to have other people weigh in on how "worldly" and "disobedient" I was to His voice for being a woman teacher. (Yeah, that accusation really happened, and that's only scratching the surface. For the longer version of that testimony, get a copy of my book *The Handmaidens Conspiracy*.)

Fourth, when I shook hands with the sound guy, he informed me that this session was going to be streamed, recorded, and added to the *56th Annual 4th of July Celebration* DVD set that had been advertised all week long…a detail nobody had mentioned when they invited me to speak. I was the keynote speaker on the biggest night of the week, during the grandest week in the year, on one of the largest networks in the history of Christian television, and every moment of it was going to be featured—irreversibly and forever—on ministry media that would be mailed all over the country.

It was too much to handle. There I was, offstage, trying not to puke or pass out while the room spun, grasping to remember what it was I had even prepared to say, refusing to let my knees buckle from fear, and forcing myself not to give in to the temptation of telling everyone I was sick and letting the studio staff figure out who was going to cover for me. My only saving grace was the fact that there were only about a hundred and fifty people gathered to hear "Donna the radical" stink up the place. All of this was on top of the fact that I had almost no experience preaching/speaking, and Jim and his audience had expectations of grandeur.

Are you with me? Are you picturing all this pressure? Can you imagine why shoving my hand in a fan sounded like a better idea than preaching at *The Prophets Speak* that day?

Okay… So, I was standing there praying for a miracle when the sound guy told me my audio set needed another battery. He meandered into a back room for a moment and came back beaming. I thought his overdone, gleeful expression was a bit much for a guy who had successfully located a battery, but before I had a chance to say a word, he blasted me.

"I just checked our streaming and we're all set up. Hey! You know how we're normally at around sixty thousand views for our *Prophets Speak* channel?"

"Uh…yeah," I said. Actually, I didn't have the foggiest idea how many views one of these presentations normally got, but as my thoughts were still bobbing around the emotionally bulldozing intimidation of the words "around sixty thousand," my mouth autonomously uttered an answer without my brain's participation or permission. The blood was already draining from my face at *that* number, and a gut feeling told me it was about to get worse.

It did.

"Well," he continued, believing that what he was about to say would be an encouragement to me, "we're expecting upwards of two million views tonight, so you will have a ton of people from all over the world hearing what you have to say! We're at 1.5 million and counting by now, all waiting for *you!*"

He was still talking, but it was like one of those scenes in a Hollywood movie when the speaker's voice trails off into the background and everything goes all slow-motion and blurry. I vaguely felt him tugging around on the wiring of my audio set as bile rose in my throat. I grabbed a decorative tree nearby—one of those pretty, lit-up trees you catch in the peripheral crowd-panning shots—and focused every cell in my body against collapsing, or vomiting, or both. When the sound guy grabbed my arm, I snapped my attention back to him midsentence.

"...like you've seen a ghost. Are you alright, Mrs. Howell? You're very pale all of a sudden."

I blinked.

"You've got this," he said, realizing the effects his previous words were having on me. "Don't worry. You're a big deal around here! You're gonna nail this. Everyone is gonna love you."

I remember, as clearly as if it were yesterday, looking out at that crowd and trying to convince myself that he would be right. God had carried me the last time these people saw me at better than my best, but even in my most articulate, confident moment, I, myself, as mere Donna Howell, couldn't compete with their expectations. They were waiting for a pulpit-on-fire, glory-hallelujah-and-amen message to detonate from the stage, fly across the room on the wings of angels, and launch a revival. They came for Popeye's post-spinach rescue act. They were about to get a flailing Olive Oyl. When God had taken over that one time in the past, I'd had my Supergirl moment, but now I was back to being Patrick Star from *SpongeBob SquarePants*.

I was a freak, and nothing short of it.

I didn't belong in this world.

Look at me, everyone, I thought to myself. *Pull out your smartphones and hit "record" because I'm about to make history. My foolhardy performance will be remixed on YouTube for ages after this. I'll go viral, and the world will remember this as the day Donna tried "preacher" on for size and the skin didn't fit…not that I ever thought it would. Maybe now I can have my cave. That sounds nice…a happy little anonymous cave.*

"You gonna be alright?" the sound man said, pulling me back to reality. "You need anything?"

I couldn't bring myself to play the sweet-and-demure card, so I blurted out the truth. "I'm very sick, I haven't slept, I forgot my notes so I'm unprepared, and I'm scared to death. These people are expecting a superstar. I can't seem to calm down and let go of this fear." When he hesitated, I smiled, deflecting with humor, which was my usual go-to. "Yeah, I'm gonna die up there. Does Jim have anything for *that* in his supplements shop?"

His first response was about what I expected to hear from any Christian. "Fear comes from the enemy." I had, of course, been given this advice countless times in the past. But then he shifted into the best—no, the only—advice that I could have absorbed or retained in that moment. "The enemy loves it when we're scared to do the Lord's work. Fear is the biggest lie. By itself, it's empty. It can't hurt you. But when you *feed* it, it grows up and devours you. Your fear, Donna, has obviously been fed for a while, and it is not something you can kill in the five minutes you have before you go onstage. You shouldn't even attempt to make it go away because that's impossible this late in the game, and the struggle of overcoming has you freezing up. So, don't *fight* the fear, *use* it." I blinked, overwhelmed at the idea that fear could be "used" for something at a time like this.

"Use it? What do you mean? I don't know what to say to them. I don't know what they want."

"First of all, don't believe what fear is telling you about yourself right now. These people just want *you*. You don't have to be anyone else. Second of all, you're afraid. That's your big issue, right? That's your opener. People love honesty, and transparency is rare. Go up there and tell them you're scared to be doing what you're doing, but you're doing it anyway because God told you to, and so can they."

The most ironic thing about his advice was that, unbeknownst to him, the sermon I had practiced to deliver was about how we should obey God despite our feelings, using Jonah as my example. Anything less than complete obedience lands us in the mouth of a fish, and when we're spat up three days later, God tells us to get back to the job He gave us, so we don't accomplish anything when we allow our feelings to direct us. Deep down, I knew that, by accepting the invitation to preach in the first place, I was being obedient to the Lord despite my feelings, but it took the sound guy to bring that to the forefront for me to see how relevant my personal weakness would be to my message.

It was perfect. I had a strong introduction now, and curiously, as soon as I knew what I was going to say, I calmed down, my stomach settled, the room-spinning subsided, I felt a boost of energy kick in, and the formerly dominating fear took a back seat: still present, but not driving. Five minutes later, I took the stage, got real with people, told them I was scared out of my mind, made everyone laugh, proceeded to preach a noteless sermon wherein I remembered every point I had practiced from the beginning, closed with a prayer, and then got the surprise of my life when my message received a third standing ovation in the Jim Bakker studio.

Another ovation.

An ovation for the freak.

The second my shoe hit the top step of the stairs on my way down from the stage, every one of my symptoms came back. I immediately became dizzy and almost fell, and I had to steady myself once again with the tree. There was a rapid barrage of nausea and an overwhelming wave of exhaustion. For some, this part of the story might sound like a bad thing, and although it wasn't my favorite thing to go through at the time, it was a detail I would never forget: physically wrecked until the moment I took to the stage, perfectly fine for forty-five minutes of preaching in front of somewhere around two million people, and then physically wrecked again the second I left the stage.

Sometimes it takes more faith to believe in a coincidence than it does a miracle. There was no doubt about it. God had carried me again.

Alone, this is one of my favorite stories to tell, because it went from anyone's worst nightmare to a great success in a matter of minutes due to what could have only been an incredible act of God. But for the purposes of this work, I explained this day at Jim's studio to show how bizarrely familiar the next scene of *The Greatest Showman* was between Barnum and Lettie. Only minutes after I had been told that I *was* the bearded lady, Lettie's character on screen is standing just behind the curtain to the circus stage, gussied up in her circus costume, preparing to face the public for the first time. From the expression on her bearded face, it's clear she is petrified to face the crowd with her "freak" showing. Although the words that Barnum gives her are different than the words the sound man gave me, the spirit of the advice—and the nature of the scene leading up to the advice—is almost identical.

BARNUM: Lettie, they're waiting.

LETTIE: For what?

BARNUM: For *you*.

LETTIE: [Nervous and reluctant, she shakes her head.] No.

BARNUM: They don't know it yet, but they are gonna love you. Trust me. [Singing:] I see it in your eyes, you believe that lie that you need to hide your face. Afraid to step outside, so you lock the door, but don't you stay that way.[5]

Once Lettie steps out into the crowd, she smiles nervously but welcomingly, and to her surprise, there are those in the gathering who smile back. The camera lingers on her face, capturing her transition from fearful to hopeful. Like I said earlier, before the curtain scene, I could already see why the Holy Spirit would present me with the bearded-lady nametag, but after seeing that her initiation onto the stage as a circus freak for the first time went down just like my initiation to the stage as the media freak, the parallel was solid as a rock. It was like God had shown me my past—summarized in the washroom scene, where Lettie reluctantly agreed to put herself out there for the world to see—and then the present "stage" Donna, who was still in the early phases of ironing out awkward wrinkles.

My popcorn was no longer a priority, as I had a sneaky suspicion that God was about to show me my future through this circus freak. How beautifully and humorously appropriate. The Lord was speaking a language that I had invented during private prayer time with Him to define me.

On the other hand, you can't imagine how nerve-wracking that was for a while. I kept thinking, *Okay, Lord. I'm watching. Gosh, I hope her character doesn't die or do something totally stupid… I want to be mature and tell You that I can take any reprimand or critique that You have for me through her character portrayal, but I would be lying if I said I wasn't a little apprehensive at this point. Will she quit the circus? And would that mean something about me quitting the formal, organized church? Please, don't let her be a knucklehead or get stabbed in an alleyway… Oh my gosh, what if she gets stabbed in an alleyway?! What in the world would You be trying to tell me with* that?

Yeah… My brain was running on an irrational treadmill, whirling and spiraling, but not actually getting anywhere productive. But despite how thoroughly I imagined every possible scenario during this fruitless mental-cardio routine, there was no preparing me for what happens later in the story. I never could have seen it coming.

A grand concert is planned around Barnum's latest addition to the show, Jenny Lind, a famous redheaded singer from Sweden. It's an enormous success, and afterward, Lettie and the rest of the circus freaks head to the back of the opera house to celebrate with Barnum amidst all his elite friends as they sip wine and hobnob. Although he had never acted ashamed of his crew before this moment, when Lettie and the others are spotted at the door, Barnum quickly intervenes to hide them away. A couple of times, Lettie tries to push past him, and he shuts the door in her face. The rejection is intense and personal, but the more important impression made in that exchange is that Lettie and her kind are just never going to fit in. She isn't going to be a part of that world. She wouldn't fit that mold no matter how hard she tried to. Her attempt to cross the threshold into the party room with the pretty people redefines the word "misfit." And I know just how she felt.

The Lord tapped me on the shoulder, and a two-second conversation sped through my mind:

HOLY SPIRIT: Are you getting this?

ME: *Oh yeah. Most definitely. I've had my share of door-slammings because I don't conform to the expectations of many in the church.*

HOLY SPIRIT: Yes, but watch what happens next…

For a moment, Lettie is devastated. As she backs away from the door and the soundtrack cues the next big musical number, I half expected her to sing a woe-is-me piece, and of course then the others would feel sorry for her or comfort her, something to that effect, and then she would find the strength to go on, etc. Sure enough, the beginning lyrics talk about how Lettie has shamefully hidden herself away from public view all her life because she is broken and valueless, and that nobody will be able to love her for what she was born to be. I thought I saw where this was going, and that I would be encouraged that I'm not alone. If that had been the whole of the message, I would have been the happiest, most touched woman in the world.

Ahem. That *wasn't* the message.

From out of the blue, Lettie looks straight ahead with newfound determination, and then calls herself and every circus freak with her "glorious."

ME: *Wait a second, Lord… GLORIOUS!?*

HOLY SPIRIT: Some people will never "fit" the mold. Some people *break* it.

I still cry to this very hour when I remember those words landing like a bomb, blowing every other thought in my head into oblivion and consuming me completely, all at the same time that Lettie sings the next unbelievable line in the song: "When the sharpest words wanna cut me down, I'm gonna send a flood, gonna drown them out. I am brave, I am bruised, I am who I'm meant to be, this is me. Look out, 'cause here I come, and I'm marching on to the beat I drum. I'm not scared to be seen. I make no apologies. This is me."[6]

"Brave," "bruised," and "what's meant to be"…all in the same concept. I was immediately reminded of a line I often say in radio and television interviews: "It's not *despite* all your bruises, your scars, and your past that God will use you, it's *because of* your bruises, your scars, and your past that you can be used!" I've said it for years, and here is Lettie, making no apologies for who she is. Her description of herself made the hair on my arms stand. She isn't attacking anyone, but she isn't going to be walked on, hidden away, or shamed for even another second. She is broken, but unstoppable; hurt, but stronger for it; perceived as a nuisance to the mainstream…

And then suddenly she's the defender of the freaks.

The newly liberated and gutsy Lettie marches straight down the hallway, every other freak trailing steadily behind her, their chins lifting a little higher with every confidence-boosting step. As they walk into an enormous ballroom filled with the rest of the privileged, aristocratic, upper-class, pinky-up, tea-drinking bluebloods, the rest of the circus group starts singing her anthem alongside her. Their body language carries a strong overtone: "I don't look like all of you, and I'm not supposed to. My value on this earth is real because I *say* it is and refuse to care if you don't agree."

By this scene, I was already a mess. I had been crying so hard that my mother (Nita Horn, as you probably know) was getting concerned. But when Lettie leads the others out of the ballroom and starts marching in the middle of the street amidst the wide-eyed stares of normal people who are offended at the mere sight of them—all the while dancing the punchiest, most crisply executed, make-way-for-the-superstars choreography I've ever seen—I added laughing and clapping to my sobbing, arriving at a smorgasbord of emotion

How convenient that the lights were out, the scene was loud, and the movie was too captivating for others in the theater to tear away from the plot of Lettie and focus on the lunatic in the fourth row...but I digress.

Lettie isn't merely going to "exist as a misfit"; she is going to "own misfit," and take the freaks with her. Because of one woman's willingness to punch the cookie cutter in the mouth, an entire community of people is empowered to face the world with each person's unique gifts and talents.

The freaks become the heroes.

So, I'm not writing this testimony today to convince any reader that I'm a hero. I have written it because I believe that *you* might be, and perhaps the only thing standing between you and your decision to embrace your God-given calling to the fullest fruition of His will is a Lettie—just one voice that's willing to reassure you: "Nope. You're not worthless. You're incredible. Believe that you're a misfit if you must, but never believe you're a mistake. You are called for such a time as this."

Have you ever felt like a misfit? I'm your Lettie. Follow me, and let's do this dance.

2

With Your Nose So Bright

By Donna Howell

Before Rudolph came along, there were only eight reindeer: Dasher, Dancer, Prancer, Vixen, Comet, Cupid, Donner, and Blitzen. This was the list provided in 1823 by American poet Clement C. Moore, most famously known for his work "'Twas the Night Before Christmas." (Actually, the real name of that poem is "A Visit from St. Nicholas," but it's so popularly known by its first line that the true title has become trivial.) Moore's poem is heavily responsible for how countless existing Christmas tradition concepts funneled into the singular Santa-and-reindeer imagery prevalent today (i.e., St. Nick smoking a pipe, having a belly like "jelly," landing on rooftops, etc.). However, the most dominant contribution to Christmas tradition by Moore has been the appearance of eight reindeer wherever Santa goes to deliver presents.

Fast forward to 1939…

The Beginning of the Red Nose

This was the year that the most ingenious publicity campaign in history was visualized by the creative marketing board at Montgomery Ward—

a famous mail-order and department store retail enterprise that dominated the Christmas season for several decades. Beginning in the early '30s, Montgomery Ward decided to give away promotional children's books to customers every holiday season. This likely wouldn't be a big deal now, but at the time, children's books were a household luxury: Unlike today's smartphone- or tablet-raised, digital-DNA generation youth, a colorful book was a beautiful present that would earn a place of honor in a child's bedroom amidst that era's comparatively technologically deficient toys. Needless to say, the scheme took off splendidly, but because the books had to be outsourced from external publishers and printers, access to books that were both new titles as well as inexpensive enough to give away was limited. (The full-color and/or hardback/board-cover formatting typical of children's books is never cheap.) So, it was decided: They would write their *own* children's book, a work of art and poetry available exclusively through Montgomery Ward, with a story surrounding a heroic Christmas character that would capture the hearts of seasonal shoppers. Doing so would not only drive consumers into the department store for that specific deal, but it would also cost Montgomery Ward far less to source the book on their own and have the gem shipped straight from the printers to their own stockrooms, cutting out book-industry middlemen costs.

Robert L. May, a low-income advertising executive of the store, was approached by his supervisor about writing the story. It needed to be uplifting, it had to appeal to a wide audience, and the central plot had to revolve around an animal of some kind. May's daughter, Barbara, had expressed a love for the deer she saw at the zoo, and there's no doubt May drew further inspiration from Moore's poem as he conceptualized a ninth reindeer being added to the previously celebrated eight. From the first line, even the rhythm of May's work follows the foundation that Moore had laid over a hundred years prior: "'Twas the day before Christmas, and all through the hills, The reindeer were playing, enjoying their spills...."[7]

Part 1: We're All Misfits Here

It was early 1939, and May would be given until late summer to have the book ready for the printer. In July, his wife Evelyn passed away from cancer, and May was told that he could abandon the project, but he refused, presenting the finished work that August and giving his mourning family something to smile about. May wrote, in a 1975 article titled "Rudolph Created in a Time of Sadness": "I needed Rudolph now more than ever. Gratefully, I buried myself in the writing. Finally, in late August [1939] it was done. I called Barbara and her grandparents into the living room and read it to them. In their eyes, I could see that the story accomplished what I hoped."[8] That following holiday season, an unbelievable 2.4 million copies of *Rudolph the Red-Nosed Reindeer* flew off department store shelves and nestled themselves under the trees of rosy-cheeked children all across the states.

The story was an immediate, high-demand classic. Overnight, the awkward reindeer was a star. Instead of becoming a tired story that declined in popularity, the buzz only grew louder in subsequent years. In 1946, the printers cranked out 3.6 million copies of the beloved colorful book that shoppers could only get at Montgomery Ward's department store at Christmas.

In 1948, May's brother-in-law, American songwriter Johnny Marks caught the Rudolph bug and wrote a song to go along with the character. After scribbling out the final piece, the infamous Gene Autry, only one of many well-known singers of his day who was approached with the proposition to perform the carol, reservedly came on board to record it for release the following Christmas of 1949. He wasn't personally a fan of Rudolph, but his wife convinced him to give the glowy-nosed deer a shot, so he reluctantly placed the song on side B of a single devoted to an unrelated song he was promoting at the time, expecting that Rudolph might gain a few bored listeners. To Autry's surprise, the single was an enormous success, and listeners hardly paid any attention to side A as fans clamored to get their hands on a copy. By the time that recording eventually sold 15 million copies,[9] ol' Gene was probably glad he took a chance.

The World of Rankin and Bass

If there had been a possibility that the poem, book, and song were going to fade from the spotlight, all that changed when *The General Electric Fantasy Hour* sponsored Rankin/Bass Productions (known at the time as Videocraft International, Ltd.) in making a stop-motion animated, made-for-television film in 1964.

The original Montgomery Ward poem/book by May involved a fairly simple plot:

- Rudolph is rejected by his peers.
- Santa is elsewhere trying to fly a sleigh through thick fog and brambles.
- Santa lands at Rudolph's house, sees his glowing nose while he sleeps, and wakes him to assist in the flight.
- Rudolph writes a note explaining that he has gone away in the middle of the night to help Santa, and when the message is found the next morning, the town gathers to await his return.
- When they get back, Santa credits Rudolph for a successful Christmas, and he's made a hero.

Because the scriptwriter, Romeo Muller, couldn't quickly attain a copy of Robert May's poem (eBay didn't exist at the time), he instead adapted the storyline off of the song, requiring some imaginative license, since that plot was even simpler than May's poem. What resulted was a complicated plot involving new elements, such as the Island of Misfit Toys, a prospector named Yukon Cornelius on the hunt for silver and gold, the threatening Bumble the Abominable Snow Monster, an elf that doesn't like to make toys (and instead wants to be a dentist), a romantic interest for Rudolph named Clarice, and a collection of other supporting characters.

Of all people, Burl Ives—at the time a country star (and now the voice of Christmas, himself, as a result of this project)—agreed to narrate the story as Sam the Snowman. His gentle timing and "grandfatherly" voiceover work was masterfully executed, lending an "all ages," "warm fireplace" feel to a work that may have otherwise come across as another adolescent Christmas kid's show. (Originally, Sam the Snowman was supposed to have a Brooklyn accent and was said to be modeled after the character Nicely-Nicely Johnson from *Guys and Dolls*, one of the great "oucha-ma-goucha," "bodda-bing, bodda-boom," cigar-chomping-type roles of that time. What good fortune that the character changed the way it did before the release!) Singing the title song was a given for Ives, but two others were added to his docket—"A Holly, Jolly Christmas" and "Silver and Gold" (originally intended to be sung by Yukon Cornelius before Ives' fame claimed the song for the Sam character)—both of which contributed to the show's instant and overwhelming reception: attention that would eventually render it "the longest-running, highest rated TV special in the history of television."[10] As the book, *The Making of the Rankin/Bass Holiday Classic: Rudolph the Red-Nosed Reindeer*, documents:

> On December 6th, 1964, as the clock struck 5:30 PM on the east coast, NBC Television beamed Rudolph out over the airwaves to tens of millions of households across the country. Back in New York, Arthur Rankin and Jules Bass could only wait and hope that their creation would appeal to America's TV viewers. The underwriters at General Electric must likewise have had their fingers crossed. When the program ended at 6:30 PM Eastern Time, the interested parties waited expectantly for the Neilsen ratings to be reported.
>
> When the ratings came in, Rankin/Bass found their show to be not just a success, but a smash hit. It had taken a 55 share for

its time slot [a share is the percentage of television sets in use]. In the years to follow, Rudolph would routinely win its time slot and consistently pull a 40–50 share. In 1995, the annual Rudolph airing on CBS garnered a 65 share.[11]

The critics followed up with a blast of positive feedback in newspapers all over the country as well, reassuring the producers of the show that it was, as would continue to be reflected in the world of media for over half a century, a worthwhile endeavor to invest in America's darling deer.

But that was then…

Things were simpler…*then*.

The Buck Stops Here

It's funny to me, watching this movie as an *adult*. As a child, so many things skimmed right over my head, and I was none the wiser about issues of political or social "correctness." Man oh man, how television has changed! Now, the things I couldn't see before are so blatant that I'm wondering how earlier generations didn't react more strongly. It certainly was, as they say, "a different era."

Before anything else is discussed, let me say that I'm actually the biggest fan of the Rankin/Bass production just under my mother, who dons her red Rudolph sweater on October first every year and doesn't take it off until the following spring. We're so big on Montgomery Ward's brainchild that it borders obnoxious.

Yeah. We're "those people." And now you've been warned.

I apologize in advance if you're one of those who has to steer your shopping cart around that enormous aisle blockade caused by the family that won't stop marveling at the latest red-nosed ornament or stuffed plush. If you find that you're getting increasingly annoyed because you can't reach the wrapping paper, check and see if the perpetrators of the bottlenecking look oddly similar to the personalities on SkyWatch Television…

The Howell residence still champions Rankin and Bass' film above all other Rudolph depictions, in part because it holds a magic that can't be recreated or imitated, but also because it *does not* spend any time overanalyzing the mental and emotional health and wellness of its characters in comparison to today's easily offended and overcomplicated concepts of psychological confidence and well-being: A young deer is born different, he gets made fun of for having that difference, and then his uniqueness saves the day. Parents are inspired, kids are encouraged, and the whole world is entertained. End of story. Moral delivered. No deep, emotional scars must be brought to light through counseling for Rudolph to be okay in the end.

Obviously, I have no problem with this movie being exactly what it is in today's world. I think sitting down to this film is the second-coolest traditional movie of the whole holiday season every year. (The first-coolest, inarguably, is the musical masterpiece *Scrooge* starring Albert Finney.) *Rudolph the Red-Nosed Reindeer* is awesome for doing precisely what it does: It represents an era marked by innocence and refreshing simplicity. Therefore, I share the following because it's amusing to note the cultural shift that's taken place since 1964, not because I find the movie offensive in any way. For those of us who grew up feeling like the Rudolph of our own story—during an age when the public is demanding an all-new level of awareness regarding social injustices such as discrimination, favoritism, and prejudice (and our media doesn't miss a chance to address that)—the Rankin/Bass production is more than just an eye-opening trip down memory lane. It leaves the more mature viewer puzzled when the characters around Rudolph are harsher to him than we remember and they don't even apologize for or get reprimanded about their harsh treatment.

In the interest of a modern reflection that leads to a meaningful take-home for readers today, I'm going to do what I just said I'm glad nobody forced this original film to do, and proceed with a deeper, more emotional and psychological analysis of this program and its characters. Like my dad said when he called me last year, once the story gets to the Island of Misfit Toys, the plot represents a timeless truth about people and God that isn't limited to 1964 children's entertainment, and the word is solid. So, stay with me while we take an otherwise perfectly executed classic and pick at it a bit through modern lenses. The end will justify the means, I assure you.

This Little Light of Mine, I'm Gonna...

The first insult occurs less than five minutes into the film when Rudolph is born. His mother and father are both instantly disgusted by their fawn's initial nose reveal, responding in such a way that suggests his uniqueness is nothing less than a revolting birth defect. The mother's response—"Well, we'll simply have to overlook it"—is only slightly less wounding than Donner's shocked retort, "Now how can you overlook *that*?!" Immediately following this conversation, Santa arrives at Donner's cave to meet the new reindeer recruit, openly acknowledging that he intends to include Rudolph on his team in the future. Then, after Santa sees the glowing red nose, he exclaims, "Great bouncing icebergs!" to which Donner quickly and nervously answers with desperate reassurance: "I'm sure it'll stop as soon as he grows up, Santa!" The next words out of Santa's mouth wouldn't last five seconds in today's politically and socially correct programming: "Well! Let's hope so if he wants to make the sleigh team someday!"[12]

Imagine that: A perceived physical flaw renders a young one's value in the magical kingdom of Christmastown completely hopeless, unless he outgrows this flaw. This precedent is a setup for failure, given that no other reindeer had ever been born with a lightbulb on his face, therefore nobody would know what steps to take to "cure" him, so he probably *will* grow up automatically eliminated from Santa's team before he ever has a chance to try out. And that conclusion is uttered from children's greatest, jolly hero of the holidays. Technically, though, a reindeer's nose is irrelevant to his ability to fly. Unless there's some underlying medical concern that Santa hasn't shared (and that would probably be too complicated to wrap a plot around in a film of this nature), a nose of a different color should not hinder this particular animal from doing that particular job, assuming he is capable of the "flying" part. This leads one to think that the only reasoning behind Santa's potential refusal to bring Rudolph onto the team someday is cosmetic.

Cosmetic!

It would have to be; what other explanation is there? A young deer has been brought into the world just minutes ago, and he's already been deemed too deformed, too unpleasant to look at, to participate in a one-night-per-year event where he would never be seen doing what he's doing anyway, since remaining hidden is part of Santa's schtick. Who would Rudolph's nose be offending or threatening, anyway? At this point, it appears that the offense truly is cosmetic, and the rejection is coming from his parents and, of all characters, Santa Claus.

But if Santa doesn't love the unlovable, who does? The motherly and fatherly acceptance and nurturing nature have already been missing from the scene, so love looks pretty far away by the time Santa voices his disinterest. Also, remember that Rudolph, though a newborn in this moment, is already talking and fully communicating with the adults in his surroundings, so it's not like these conversations about his uselessness are happening when he's too young to understand the rejection. These words about his "defect" are happening right in front of him.

If only it had been limited to the beginning of the film… But alas, it gets worse.

So, anyway, Santa sings his happy "Jingle, Jingle, Jingle" number, identifying himself as king, and leaves the cave without a word. Donner, clearly embarrassed and ashamed of Rudolph's abnormality, faces his new son directly and says, "Oh, Santa's right! You'll *never* make the sleigh team!" Donner's spirits, however, are quickly lifted when he gets struck with the bright idea to cover Rudolph's nose in mud to trick everyone into thinking he's "normal"—a "chip off the old antlers" like the rest of them, he says. Now, only after Rudolph's defect is hidden, Donner shows his boy some paternal affection. The scene cuts to narrator Sam the Snowman, who has the audacity to call Rudolph's nose a "noncon-formity," as if the little deer purposefully set out to oppose the acceptable ways of his community by being born with a peculiar body part.[13]

A few minutes later, because the first muddy nose covering doesn't last, the audience rejoins Donner, his wife, and Rudolph in the privacy of their cave as Donner produces a newer, more improved model of the fake nose, because he is "determined to keep Rudolph's nose a secret," Sam says.

DONNER: Alright, Son, try it on.

RUDOLPH: I don't wanna. Daddy, I don't like it.

DONNER: [harshly:] You'll *like* it and *wear* it!

RUDOLPH: Aww, but Daddy... [Midsentence, a hoof flies in from the right side of the screen, forcefully shoving the fake nose onto Rudolph's face, despite his protestations. Rudolph's voice becomes nasal—much like the sound of your voice when you try to talk while holding your nose closed—and the awkward, cumbersome fit of the prosthetic instantly impedes Rudolph's ability to speak clearly, as his next words can only barely be made out.] It's not very comfortable.

DONNER: There are more important things than comfort: self-respect![14]

Let's look at the implications that we've accumulated so far from this warmhearted classic: a) perceived birth defects equal shame on the parents, shame on the community leader, and shame on the unfortunate soul who is born different; b) the *victim* will be blamed for this blemish when prominent spokespeople in his environment openly identify it as a "nonconformity" (as if it's something he can control); c) the victim is taught to hide his imperfection from the world around him—up to and including inhumane concealment tactics that restrict his breathing and cause speech impediments—lest he risk losing his "self-respect."

Hide it under a bushel? Uh, no…

How, as children, did we never see that all these support characters around Rudolph are such bullies? It's quite a trip.

After leaving his cave alone and lonely, Rudolph sings the first round of the intermittently woven theme song "Misfit," and shortly after, the reindeer games are off to a swell beginning, thanks to the cruel prosthetic nose Donner fashioned to keep the wool over everyone's eyes. Meanwhile, the cut scene of the elves dedicating their latest act of affection for their leader—a song called "We Are Santa's Elves"—is met with an angry, inconvenienced Santa who is ticked that he has to sit through their ditty while the new deer are waiting for him.

Seriously. Watch it again if you don't remember this scene. Santa acts like a total jerk. When the chief elf foreman over the toy factory announces that they have worked tirelessly on a performance for him, he literally slumps down in his throne and says, "Let's get this over with," and then pouts, jeers, sighs, wriggles about, and taps his fingers impatiently on his armrest until the end of the song. Then, unbelievably, he responds to their demonstration of love and devotion with a curt, "Hmm, well, it needs work. I have to go."[15]

When I brought this to the attention of my brother (Joe Horn) a few years ago, he wouldn't believe it at first, and when I pulled up the scene on YouTube so he could see it for himself, he couldn't stop laughing. "Wow! The things you *don't* see as a kid!" he said. "Why in the world is he all grumbly? What's his problem?"

After a few more comments from Joe about how Santa needed to take "an enormous dose of chill," I directed his attention to a much more surprisingly insensitive display later in the film.

Back at the games, Rudolph meets Clarice, who tells him right away that he talks funny, but then makes the redeeming comment that she thinks he's cute. This leads to the adorable and iconic "I'm cuuuuuute!" outburst that shows, for the first time to the audience, Rudolph's high proficiency as a potential sleigh reindeer when he leaps into the air and nails an expert landing. Based on the reindeer that had gone just before him and Coach Comet's acknowledgment that the deer's clumsy face plant is an excellent performance for a first try, it's clear that nobody has seen anything like Rudolph. He jumps again several times and wows everyone on the scene. Unfortunately, Rudolph's excitement over the pretty doe also leads to wrestling with another little buck. His nose's disguise comes unhinged, revealing his shameful "nonconformity" and sending all the reindeer around him into mocking hysterics. He stands in the center of the circle while the rest take turns humiliating and ridiculing his glowing nose, calling him mean names and ganging up on him.

It's at this nightmare moment that my adult mind is, once again, completely blown, when Santa displays the worst reaction conceivable. Instead of coming to the victim's defense and focusing on Rudolph's brilliant launch-and-landing demonstration, Santa publicly berates Rudolph's father: "Donner, you should be ashamed of yourself! What a pity. He had a nice takeoff, too." As if that's not bad enough, when Coach Comet blows his whistle to call the bucks-in-training to the next round of practice, Rudolph turns to join his peers, and Comet stops him in his tracks. He announces to the entire assembly that, from then on, Rudolph will be forbidden to participate in any reindeer games. "Right?" Comet says to everyone present, calling for their unanimous approval. "Right!" they all say, banding together against Rudolph, corporately banishing him from having any place within the community.[16]

Once again, my brother Joe found this unbelievable: "What in the world?! Donner should be ashamed of himself because his son has a birth defect?"

"Well, I dunno," I countered. "It might have been because he tried to hide it from everyone at the games?"

"No, Santa already knew of Rudolph's nose. He saw it in the cave. Why would he see Rudolph's takeoff, get all excited, and *then* get angry at Donner when his fake nose falls off in front of everyone?"

I considered this for a second. "Maybe because Donner promised him that he would grow out of it, so Santa saw the false black nose and thought he had? It would make sense why Santa would be deceived like the rest and then—"

"Yeah, but," Joe interrupted, "you're assuming anyone in the audience would pick up on that. That's too intricate and complex a plot for a movie that is otherwise blatantly simple."

"Good point. I have no idea why Donner should be ashamed in this scene." I looked down at the screen and laughed. "Maybe we just have to chalk it up to 'times were different then'? There appears to be no other explanation for why a father should be publicly humiliated by the 'king' of the land because his son is born different, *or* that Rudolph isn't allowed to fly because of a nose issue, or for that matter, why anyone assumes that a flashlight nose is a negative thing to begin with. That could be handy, right?"

"So…but if Donner…" Joe blinked. "Wait—banishment, though? Permanent exclusion from the community outdoor recreation center and all of its games? For the glowy-nose thing? That's a bit extreme." Joe tried for a moment to piece the unreasonable characters' reactions together, then shook his head in resignation with a laugh. "Whatever. Santa's a blockhead."

I agreed.

As readers are aware, the rest of the story involves Rudolph's choice to run away, followed up with his meeting Hermey—the elf who would rather be a dentist than make toys, and is therefore, himself, a fellow misfit within his own toy-factory community. Together, and eventually alongside the semi-creepy pickaxe-licker, Cornelius, Rudolph and Hermey stumble upon the Island of Misfit Toys, and the rest is history: Rudolph eventually returns home to face his fears, Santa cancels Christmas because of the fog, and Rudolph-with-his-nose-so-bright makes gift delivery possible again. With Christmas back on, the movie ends with Rudolph as a hero…

…despite what everyone told him he'd amount to, and

…regardless of what vicious voices attempted to tear him down and trample him under.

All this in the face of a perceived "ugly" mark, and heedless of the "birth defect" or "disability."

Rudolph saved Christmas with the very feature everyone thought would disgrace it.

Consider that the next time your own "broken part," whatever that is in your life, stares you down and tells you you're worthless. It just might be the feature that brings the greatest glory when least expected.

A Hero for Grace, Not a Nose

But let's not allow the superficial "nose" element to be the last word on this story. That, by far, is not the bottom line. Look at how this whole thing goes down…

After Rudolph is inaugurated into Santa's elite, in an ironically familiar steering of events, all the other characters jump on the suddenly supportive bandwagon, instantly and conveniently befriending yesterday's outcast, clapping and cheering for the miracle of the red nose. Nobody apologizes or stands corrected. Those responsible for participating in the ostracization of—and injury to—an innocent soul for superficial and egocentric reasons are now allowed to join the celebration of the miracle nose they once hated without any social awkwardness or consequence of any kind.

How could they possibly have the right? Where's the justice?

In all fairness, as stated earlier, this *was* 1964, and storytelling was a completely different animal at that time. You could have the Santa of the story praise the Rudolph once at the end and it "fixes" everything.

Part 1: We're All Misfits Here

The "I was wrong, please forgive me" scene wasn't necessary because it was assumed in the triumphant observance of the outcast-turned-hero. Americans weren't so quick to get offended about any little thing, so Rankin and Bass got away with depicting various increasing levels of public shame, harassment, oppression, and outright discrimination upon a character whose only offense is that he was born.

If done correctly—if these tormenters were to be shown from the beginning of the film to be detestable bad guys—a modern production company might be culturally permitted to involve them in a film today, but it would have to be obvious from the beginning credits that they are the "unlikeables" instead of the endearing mothers, fathers, peers, and holiday leaders who swoop in at the end and pretend they were never jerks. They would have to, at some point, face correction and show remorse, or face exile themselves. Anything less, if this movie were made today, would make our current political climate blow up, likely resulting in a #Red-NosedLivesMatter viral fallout.

I personally wouldn't change a thing, however. There have been a lot of box office duds in the last fifteen years because a simple kids' movie was overcomplicated with "deep-emotional-scar" psychological analyses that go above a child's head anyway. In these cases, who is the movie made for? At the end, kids are bored and parents are depressed. So, although I can, as an adult in this current world, pick up on moments of abandonment, neglect, and community-wide victimization of an undeserving soul in *Rudolph* that flew over my head as a child, I can also be realistic about the cultural shift and see that the folks over at the Rankin/Bass studio were motivated only to raise up Rudolph. If we allow a reasonable perspective, we can all remember that this endearing classic ultimately empowered the underdogs, and never endorsed the cold-shouldering of them.

That said, there is a reason people connect with Rudolph, and it's about so much more than a nose. A schnozzle-that-saves-Christmas tale isn't something any person can claim as his or her own story, and high fives around a toy factory just before Santa's flight wouldn't reverse the psychological damage of a lifetime's worth of bullying and neglect.

No, the reason people feel they have something in common with Rudolph is because they see themselves with a broken feature—something that hasn't been right for as long as they can remember, a "flaw" that makes them undesirable, ostracized, or rejected. They relate to the moment the red-nosed reindeer's family wants to love him but can't; to the moment his peers embrace him, then see his blemish, and kick him to the curb; and to the moment that even the greatest hero in their local history refuses to let him amount to anything so long as his "shortcoming" can't be hidden away.

"Hide what you are, or go it alone." That's the message the people feel, and that's why they relate to the one unlovable misfit who rose above the odds.

Then, there's Rudolph's response to all the drama. That is a high-bar standard that each of us innately (even if it's deep, deep down) wants to match. We may act tough, have trust issues, fear the repeat offense, or put up protective walls, but at the core of every soul, God instills the desire to be good, kind, amiable, and gracious.

Let's put a real-life spin on this: If Rudolph were a real character, and if his story were true, you would likely be looking at some major commotion in Christmastown in the days following his climb to the top of the social ladder. Eventually, he would probably develop mommy and daddy issues requiring family counseling in a neutral environment wherein Rudolph could ask, point blank, "Why didn't you love me from birth? Why was something as trivial as my nose a reason for you to reject me? Why did I have to be pronounced the deliverer from Christmas fog for you to look at me without disdain and shame?" More likely than not, the same reindeer fellows who tease him and make him feel worthless before would return to their superficial and backstabbing nature after a while, jealously spewing that Rudolph "isn't any better than the rest" of them, and "if it weren't for his ridiculous red nose," they could be "at the front of the reins," etc. Would a doe with Clarice's personality stay with Rudolph under the pressure of all that attention? Or would she stray from him for a quieter life with another reindeer? A Santa like this one—who doesn't have the time of day for his most devoted staff and who will only work his charity when he's surrounded by cosmetic perfection—can't be relied on for any real integrity. Being his top-tiered, prized employee would most certainly result in a nightmarish clash of personalities if Rudolph miraculously managed to stay the humble, sweet, honest buck that he is when the movie ends.

And what of Rudolph, himself? Could he ever be happy in the lime-light, since his entire existence is in the darkness of solitude and shame? Could he even adjust to something like that, realistically, without losing his mind? Would he, like real people in the world who have lived the from-zero-to-hero role, feel that all the "love" he is receiving on the other side of the nose debacle is paper thin and artificial since it wasn't there *before* he was put in the hall of fame as a result of a glowing nose he didn't ask for or earn?

Because we are fallen in our humanity, the gracious and humble way that Rudolph handles himself at the film's close appears anticlimactic. It only works because it's TV. If this story was true (obviously involving humans and not talking animals), we would crave more justice for him than this, and we might even desire the story to end with his revenge against oppressors. But, if you entertain that thought for a moment, you can see why the "human" ending ruins the whole...

*And, within this thread of thought, we can identify the **true** source of Rudolph's heroism!*

Go there in your thoughts for a quick minute. If *Rudolph the Red-Nosed Reindeer* concluded with Rudolph having a meltdown, making demands, becoming cynical, displaying an attitude problem, using his celebrity status to make everyone pay, or graduating from misfit to manipulator—*if this happened even on a tiny scale*—it would contaminate the beauty of the story. The whole tale would become another "retaliation and payback" epic, if not just a terrible ending. Sure, people might feel a corporate, "Haha, you had it comin'" shout rise within their spirits, and I admit that might even bring them temporary joy, but only as it feeds their internal, fallen hunger for vengeance. No lesson could be learned from an ending like that, and Rudolph would most definitely not be hailed a hero. In fact, at best, he'd remain a perpetual victim.

In the end, it is never about the nose, the glowing, the fog, the oppression, or even the misfit. None of these is a "save-the-day" factor, because all of these fail to mean a thing if Rudolph doesn't conduct himself with grace. Rudolph is not the savior of anything because he came into the world with a bizarre nose. It's his character that makes the story. He saves the day with integrity, humility, forgiveness, and confidence moving forward, letting the past go in trade for a bright future involving anyone who wants to tag along.

It's by his mercy toward others that Rudolph becomes the redeemer: All the other characters are granted a second chance in their Christmas-town calling because one adorable little reindeer says resentment and justice aren't as important as family uniting for the common goal of charity. Children all over the world are waiting for that blessing under the tree, that reason to smile on Christmas morning, and Rudolph doesn't even blink when it's time for him to soar past the bitterness of previous offense and into the great commission of his season: "Go ye into all the world, through the fog, and distribute gifts to every creature."

See, Rudolph can't bicker or delay Christmas with his drama or past hurt. He can't bring himself to, because he has people to bless and minister to. Children are depending on him to play his important part in completing a work far grander than himself, for a purpose far grander than himself, and he is gracious and faithful in making them the priority over his own finite circumstances.

Poetry in motion.

But see, here's something you probably didn't know: Not everyone in the original 1964 audience was happy with the first Rankin/Bass ending...

Part 1: We're All Misfits Here

This was expressed by an army of angry viewers who organized an official, public, letter-writing campaign in the weeks following that very first 1964 airing. So many complaints and protestations poured in demanding that the writers fix the ending of the film that the producers felt they had no choice but to concede, giving the audience what they wanted. The entire crew had to be reassembled, including the stop-animation puppeteers from Tokyo, who had to fly back out and fire up all the cameras for a tedious recreation of the last several minutes of the movie. What an ordeal!

(As an interesting and hilarious side note: When the ending was tweaked, we lost a scene wherein Yukon Cornelius finally strikes it rich by throwing his ice pick into the snow below and uncovering a "peppermint mine," which secretly has been his heart's desire throughout the film up to this point, as opposed to silver and gold [although the audience has no way of knowing it yet]. This "peppermint mine" scene is the only explanation for why this character repeatedly and aggressively licks his ice pick every time he strikes any surface throughout the movie. However, after this scene was cut to make room for the alternate ending, Cornelius' constant tonguing of his mining tool has been, for generations…well, weird and creepy. Only in the last few major releases of the film has this scene been resurrected, restoring the prospector's sanity.)

Was this public backlash because the ending was unrealistic? No, because people never have required an ending to be realistic, or even to tie up all loose ends. Was it due to the fact that Rudolph never receives closure or an apology from those who hurt him? No, because, again, it was 1964, and that closure was coupled with Santa hailing Rudolph as a hero. Was it because Rudolph doesn't stand up for himself or get revenge? No, because such behavior wouldn't be in keeping with his kind, gracious, and forgiving character.

So, what was the problem?

Glad you asked…

No Toy Left Behind

The 1964 version ended when Santa and Rudolph flew into the sky, *failing to make good on the promise of returning to the Island of the Misfit Toys*. The sudden credits surprised viewers of all ages who had been waiting through the second half of the film to receive closure on the fate of the unlovables. When there was no definite resolution for the sad dolly, the train with the square wheels, the Charlie-in-the-Box, or the rest of them, despite Rudolph's oath to care for his fellow misfits…the hero became the abandoner.

As history does tell, the producers over at the Rankin/Bass Studio responded favorably to the letter campaign and viewer demands. The new ending, which involved Santa and Rudolph returning to the island to distribute the lonely toys to loving children all over the globe, satisfied the world.

Note something interesting here: The public *could* have been outraged that the parents never loved the small deer. They *could* have been mad that Santa, himself, saw only disability and limitation. They *could* have railed against Comet for banishing the team's best flyer for an aesthetic and unrelated purpose. They *could* have written in that at least one of the little reindeer's parents at the games gave their offspring a stern lecture on love and acceptance instead of allowing their kid to blast out-of-control mockery at an isolated and hurting child. They *could have carried out a number of protestations against this film*.

But they didn't. All these issues were given closure. Instead, they banded together to make the statement: The "misfits," the "broken," the "unlovables" cannot and will not be left behind and forgotten. This was a grievance too much to tolerate.

And for whom did these people really rise up? A bunch of fictional toys in a stop-animation movie? Certainly not. That's silly. The underlying motivation behind their activism was for real-life misfits. If we allow a representative character to get the shaft, our silence stands as an endorsement that we are okay with allowing the world to forget those of us who feel the way these sad toys did. No, the campaign wasn't for the "toys."

They protested on behalf of all who feel they don't belong. They made a stance for the broken, the disabled, the lonely. They broadcast with their actions that no one is left behind in this game of life; *every soul* has value, and there is no toleration or appreciation for the insinuation that those the world deems as damaged goods won't be allowed to share in the happy ending. They rose up for every odd man out, every loner, anyone mislabeled as a "nonconformist."

They did it for you, and they did it for *me*, the bearded-lady freak.

You, with your nose so bright, let it shine, let it shine, let it shine…

Part 2

The Floating Misfit

In a book that, by design, leans on an understanding of misfit toys, it seems only natural that one of our main objectives would be to examine each of these oddballs and reveal precisely why he or she was an outcast. Additionally, finding a way to somehow redeem their standing back into society may seem as though it would rapidly fall into our list of objectives. While the first may be somewhat true—as we will explore the eccentricities of each of these creatures—there will be no effort to "fix" them. Instead, we wish to assert each of their peculiarities as unrecognized strengths that an individual has chosen to view instead as a handicap, or to point out that some of these are actually no different from others, and that his or her conviction that they are different and thus nonconformist is actually the entire summation of their problem.

And yet, as has been mentioned, the television-viewing world of the 1960s was so unwilling to leave these outsiders behind that expensive, time-consuming (at its time) production was restarted just to meet the public's demands of resolve for these exiles. Why? Because, when the truth is told, each of us sees a little of ourselves in the reflection of these beings. And, as such, each understands that if the fate of these is left unexamined and unsettled, it makes the silent statement that misfits everywhere don't matter and are not worth saving. This isn't a conclusion that an entire population of self-perceived oddballs will take sitting down, so the demand that the fate of the toys be redeemed actually reflects our own desire for reconciliation, redemption, and recognition of our inner value. And, this is evidence that there is a spiritual component to our banishing perception toward both others and ourselves. Since, deep down, those who stand for the rejected ones are not fictional characters, but are actual human beings with noble and innate desires, perhaps before moving on to study the toys, we should visit a real-life example of one of the greatest misfits of all time. Rest assured that we will return to these outcast playthings and cover them at length, but first, let's take an in-depth look at a misfit you thought you knew, but likely had no idea just what an oddball he truly was.

This nonconformist is the one who washed up in a basket…

3

The Baby in a Basket

By Donna Howell, Allie Henson, and Nita Horn

Some might be wondering why we chose to use Moses instead of Jesus as our example of the "ultimate misfit." Our Messiah was, in fact, a supreme misfit among those of His day, wasn't He?

As a matter of fact—cold, hard, historical *fact*—He was.

Considering the sheer volume of prophecies He fulfilled in His coming, you wouldn't think so…but it's no secret that the Jews wanted Him to arrive like a military champion to free them from the oppression of Rome. (And, had He been what they wanted, it might have fixed an uncomfortable wrinkle in time for the Jewish nation, but it would have been a travesty of unending proportion if that temporary, earthly goal was all He had come to accomplish.) When He didn't take down Rome, their continual discomforts related to social and political affairs led them to reject Him as the Promised One. He met their challenges and provocations time and time again with answers that have forever blessed this world, showing wisdom and restraint that no regular human will ever equal or surpass…but these answers infuriated the religious leaders of His day when He did not concede and give them what they wanted, so He became even more a misfit to *His own people.*

By the time Jesus was taken to trial, He had more than proved Himself to be the Son of God to anyone who had eyes to see and ears to hear (such as His throngs of disciples), but He would never soothe the grandiose expectations of those who cried "Crucify him!" from the crowds.

In light of the eternal plan, Jesus' death was no tragedy. But in His day, for those who didn't believe, Jesus, the grandest misfit of human history, would be hung on a cursed tree to die like a criminal.

Talk about a Man who punched the legalistic Jews' cookie-cutter-Messiah mold in the mouth!

Nevertheless, there are two major reasons we opted to focus on Moses instead:

1. At the end of the day, and in the context of this book, "misfit" relies on the idea that we feel inadequate and need a little shove to feel worthy of those grand events in our future toward which we've been called, and Jesus didn't feel inadequate. He knew since Creation who He was and what He would do.
2. None of us will ever feel like Jesus or be able to compare ourselves to Him. Though He is the number-one subject that Christians should be studying, when it comes to materials like this book that seek to find another finite, fallen human we can relate to, it would be doing the Son of God a disservice to suggest that specific kind of resemblance.

And, yes, we know that God chose to send His Son in wholly human, wholly God form in part so we humans would find Him easier to relate to, but the context is different. As merely one of many theological examples: We are blessed in finding Him relatable because He was "tempted in every way just as we are" (Hebrews 4:15). Now, any time we face temptation, no matter what it is, we can say that our Savior knows how that feels. That's excellent, wonderful, amazing news that the very God of the universe who created everything, including emotion, would be able to connect with us in such a personal way! It shoots down the idea that God is some faraway being who made us and set us in motion, then just sits back and watches us bungle around, choosing to be uninvolved with our lives and pain (that's the god of deism, by the way)... The benefits of Jesus having been tempted could go on for a hundred pages or more!

But...

He did *not* sin. Ever. He never allowed Himself to participate in any moral failing (Hebrews 4:15). And, as much as we hate to say it, we can't relate to that. We human misfits, in part, feel the way we do because of imperfections that we don't have in common with Christ. And what good would it do to write a book that states, "God will not only use you *despite* your flaws, He will use you *because of* your flaws!" and then give you the Flawless One as the example? One of the central purposes of this book is to encourage those who identify as misfits, oddballs, eccentrics, and loners to rise into the calling God has placed on their lives and obey what He is asking them to do, even when they don't believe they will ever be qualified. Jesus cannot and will not ever be categorized as one who failed, delayed, or even questioned what the Father was asking of Him, and in this way, He did not and does not identify as a misfit. In this area—one that is crucial to this book—no human alive will ever be, *nor should ever be*, capable of identifying with Jesus' perfection this side of eternity.

Yet, for readers who've never really thought about Jesus as a *societal* misfit: Consider all He was to His peers and the religious people of His day; think of how bizarre He must have looked to those in the secular world of His day, too. Then be immensely encouraged by the fact that His story is a blazing example (among many martyrs in Church history) of how obedience to God's call on a life can change the world forever.

If Jesus could rise to the occasion, if His disciples and apostles could follow His example, and if passionate men and women all over the world since the time of the apostles could give their whole lives over to "the call," no matter what the cost, following *their* examples…then so can *you*.

Oh, also…so did Moses. His obedience cost him everything, even up to the very end. And, remember how we said that Jesus was perfect? Moses wasn't.

This Study Is *Not* What You Think

Before we begin our look at Moses, we want to stress one thing: *This is not your average study on the life of Moses!* It's not even close. You won't be reading about the ten plagues of Egypt; Pharaoh's repeated refusals to let Moses' people go; the theology of whether each of the plagues was a judgment upon a specific god of the Egyptian pantheon; the parting of the "Red" Sea (by the way, this really should be "Reed Sea," named for the reeds that grew in and around it, not for Moses/God turning the water into blood, because that happened at the Nile River, roughly 450 miles away as a bird flies); the delivery of the Ten Commandments on stone tablets at Mt. Sinai; the worship of a golden calf that angered Moses and made him break the stone tablets; the ironic grumbling of slaves who wanted to return to captivity because they didn't fancy Canaan; the forty years of wandering to complete a trip that should have taken a few weeks; or any other major Moses-ism celebrated in our culture. In fact, our character study here will start from the beginning and carry through only to Moses' encounter with the burning bush.

We're not refraining from looking at these events and topics because discussions about them have been exhausted or because they're unimportant. It's because they've been well covered by many other qualified authors—and, frankly, these are parts of the story of Moses that almost everyone in the Church already knows.

What we look at here is probably nothing like anything you'll ever see in another book. Using Moses as one example (a powerful one), we're attempting to debunk a few misconceptions about the lives and identities of Bible characters. (Wait, did we say a *few* misconceptions? Sorry… we meant a ton!)

One thing we've found tragic in the Church, the Body of Christ, is that very few believers know the truth behind what is documented in the Word regarding the men and women whose life stories help lead us in being faithful Christians today. And it's great that we do find help in their example! For instance, after experiencing a blip of doubt in our walk with God and feeling terrible about ourselves as a result, we can recall the example of the Apostle Peter and think, *Well, he denied Christ three times on the night of His arrest, so I guess I'm alright for having those thoughts and feelings the other day.* We can draw strength from these real-life people who made real-life mistakes, and whose real-life attitudes showed that they, too, identified as misfits, unworthy of the call of God. When we see them rise above their own self-doubt, it encourages us, and that's one of the main benefits their stories provide.

But how many of us can say we really understand who these people were? This side of eternity, before we're allowed to break bread with them ourselves and get to know them, that's always going to remain a challenge to some extent, certainly. However, we think it's our duty to try to understand—to the best of our abilities—Scripture and the lives that established that Living Book in the first place.

Unfortunately, the Church is becoming more and more used to "Xerox theology." If you've read some of Donna's works, you will understand what that means. For those of you who haven't, think about making a copy of an original picture. Now, take the copy and make another copy. Then, take the most recent copy and make another from that. Eventually, so many copies later, the clarity of the original is lost forever, unless someone finds the original image and insists that everyone looks at only the first, genuine portrayal. Likewise, at some point throughout history, every story gets "Xeroxed" one too many times, and the truth is lost until someone finds the original and insists that everyone hears only the first, genuine version recorded. (Oh, dear Lord! Have you read the original fairy tales we tell our kids? They are gruesome and bloody! These authors prefer them over the Disney-ized versions, in the same way we prefer the actual Bible over cartoons about stories from Scripture, but wow! Reading what was *first* written can be a trip sometimes.)

In the case of Bible characters, the closer we can get to what was really recorded about them—not "cartoon" variety folks whose depth only goes to the bottom of a peanut shell—the more we can absorb, apply, and relate to who they really were. And since "all scripture is given by inspiration of God, and is profitable for doctrine, for reproof, for correction, for instruction in righteousness" (2 Timothy 3:16), the examples set by the people in the pages are there to instruct us how to live, not just to provide us with entertaining stories. Yet, if we are to live in a way that reflects our knowledge of these men and women, then we need to know them—for "reals," not for "fakes."

Our goal in this study is therefore to strip away "Xerox Moses" and replace him with the real guy whose life probably looks nothing like how it's depicted in the movies you've seen, the books you've read, or the way his story is typically (mis)interpreted. Keep in mind as you go that, although we've chosen Moses to make a powerful point, he is only one of many misfits of the Bible whose stories we could have featured to this degree. Had we chosen to do that, our book would be longer than the Bible, but we want you to carry this thought with you: For every moment that you feel encouraged or motivated by seeing that God used an oddball like Moses, of all people, to do the amazing things he did (trust us, you will have those thoughts when you begin to see his real situation), there are tons of other examples throughout the Word of God using surprising people in surprising ways.

Part 2: The Floating Misfit

We've Been Through the Desert with a Man of No Name?

Now here's a character who, from the beginning, flies off the paper like a man doomed to failure and never-ending oddball-isms. If you recall, he was never even supposed to be born.

In the Disney film, *A Bug's Life*, the leader of the grasshoppers—oh-so-originally named "Hopper" (whose idea was that?)—realizes the tiny ants outnumber the larger grasshoppers by a landslide. Despite the one-on-one size difference—the grasshopper, of course, towering over the ant—Hopper acknowledges that if the ants ever had a mind to, they could easily band together and squash the entire grasshopper community, leaving them without their giant sea of ant slaves. Hopper's solution is to increase the oppression over the ant community, demoralizing them in the process, and keep himself established as king over all bugdom. But the harsher conditions of Hopper's domination backfire when the ants, who continue to multiply, are triggered to fight back.

(Spoiler alert: The ants win at the end of the movie. Why and how? Because a misfit ant—a totally embarrassing outcast named Flik whose quirky, "time-saving" inventions always malfunction and result in catastrophe—outplays the grasshoppers with his wit and intelligence, and *then* rises up as a brave war leader when the battle comes to blows. Hopper meets his end when one of Flik's now-genius inventions [a fully operational bird fashioned from leaves and twigs] tricks him into provoking a real bird, who retaliates by offering Hopper as baby food for her nest of fluffy, yellow hatchlings. As it turns out, the eccentricity that has ostracized Flik from his community early on is the very quirk that saves his people…er, *colony*, rather. Are you starting to see the recurring theme? Misfits who break the mold have valuable gifts and ideas that, with the right timing and circumstances, save the day. Just another quick plug for the misfits. Now back to Moses…)

At the beginning of the book of Exodus, we see a new king rise to the throne over Egypt. At least as far as the biblical narrative follows, the first move the new ruler makes is to pull *A Bug's Life*-style, Hopper-istic, oppress-the-ants stunt, drawing up enormous blueprints for the cities Pithom and Raamses, establishing Israelite labor camps with a sea of slaves, and appointing cruel Egyptian slave drivers over them:

> Now there arose up a new king over Egypt... And he said unto his people, "Behold, the people of the children of Israel are more and mightier than we: Come on, let us deal wisely with them; lest they multiply, and it come to pass, that, when there falleth out any war, they join also unto our enemies, and fight against us, and so get them up out of the land."
>
> Therefore they did set over them taskmasters to afflict them with their burdens. And they built for Pharaoh treasure cities, Pithom and Raamses.
>
> But the more they [Egyptians] afflicted them, the more they [Israelites] multiplied and grew.... And the Egyptians made the children of Israel to serve with rigour: And they made their lives bitter with hard bondage, in morter, and in brick, and in all manner of service in the field: all their service, wherein they made them serve, was with rigour. (Exodus 1:8–14)

As it's relevant to a later, crucial moment in the story of Moses (and therefore important to have in the back of our minds from the beginning), we'll take a moment to look at what a "taskmaster" is here, as it could be slightly misleading to a modern reader (especially to those who are newer to Bible reading or who stick to only one translation). This word just doesn't mean what it used to.

At times, "slavery" in the Bible refers to a more peaceful and mutual agreement between "slave" and master, resembling concepts of indentured servitude from recent Western history. It's more of a "Butler Jeeves" thing in certain ancient cultures, despite the translations favoring "slave" over a more accurate depiction in today's world (like what the word "servant" might imply). For example, this voluntary arrangement is present in the Deuteronomy passages dealing with how Israelite slave owners are to treat their slaves, and which heavy consequences will befall owners found mistreating their slaves. (Look to chapters 15–21 for a wider and more accurate context. This section of Scripture has been mangled by aggressive nonbelievers who, in light of recent social and political shifts, have started referring to these laws as "God's instructions on how to beat your slave." They pluck single verses and even partial verses out and away from their fuller context, completely missing the point that, when read altogether, this section of the Bible is "God's instructions on how much and what kind of punishment will be enacted upon slave owners who beat their slaves"—and the "slave," of course, in this context, is a Jew of the same race who has taken a *paid position* to work under a housemaster voluntarily as his full-time job.) This demand of kindness cancels out the idea that every instance of the word "slave" in the Bible is going to point to harsh treatment, so the language-barrier line is sometimes blurred between a "Jeeves" concept and the reality of intensely oppressed men and women being beaten into submission with whips. That is why it begs clarification here that what we're talking about in Exodus is the *latter* of these two ideas.

More accurately within the context of Exodus, "taskmaster" should read "slave drivers" if it is to have the correct effect. One commentary explains that "*mas* (translated 'task') was a technical term in Israel for 'forced labour,'" and notes that "such taskmasters were hated [as] can be seen from the stoning of Adoram later (1 Kgs 12:18)."[17] Another shows that the purpose of the ancient Egyptian taskmaster over the Israelite was to "enslave and maltreat them...[with] whips—to punish the indolent, or spur on the too languid."[18] So, yes, we are literally talking about God's people being whipped and beaten, to the point that they had open sores festering under the hot sun, if they didn't build the pagan king's supply centers fast enough.

A third commentary helps us understand the king's otherwise ambiguous logic: "It was hoped that severe labour under the lash would produce so much suffering that the number of the Israelites would be thinned, and their multiplication stopped."[19] Against today's backdrop, with cushy air conditioning and fluffy couches waiting to greet most in the West after a long day, it's even more difficult to imagine that hard labor would be a national ruler's bright idea of population deterrence, but it's more conceivable when we imagine what the Israelites were up against in that day. Alas, the guy was daft enough to try it...

As a result, because God was ultimately in control, Israel increased all the more.

When the king's first attempt at intimidating, demoralizing, or depopulating the Israelites met with dismal failure, he traded in his Disney grasshopper role for an eerie Hitler impression—Plan B was pure, unadulterated genocide:

And the king of Egypt spake to the Hebrew midwives... And he said, When ye do the office of a midwife to the Hebrew women, and see them upon the [child-birthing] stools; if it be a son, then ye shall kill him. (Exodus 1:15–16)

Moses wasn't even supposed to live beyond the birthing stool. If not for the intervention of the power of God through the suddenly emboldened midwives, the "story of Moses" would have been "Moses was born to a Hebrew woman named Jochebed, then he died." But the midwives couldn't bear following through with the evil Pharaoh's plans to destroy the life that God created, so he was slipped back into his mother's arms, where he stayed in secret for three months.

Though the Word does not describe it, we know from the desperation Jochebed showed in keeping Moses alive that she was driven by a maternal nature to care for her baby. We can therefore assume that Moses was given a Hebrew name—and don't miss how significant this is! Hopefully by now, most are aware of how important genealogy was to the Jews. Even from the very beginning with Adam and Eve, the people of God always kept painstaking records of who was whose child (as we now see in the "son of…son of…son of" sections of Scripture). Likewise, most genealogies focus on the males in the family tree, and the names of males would live on forever, so those names were important details. In the earliest of known Jewish traditions, "a person's name is thought to define and control his or her soul and destiny (Ber[achot] 7b). Therefore, the selection of an appropriate name is a critical decision."[20]

"Moses," Hebrew *Moshe*, means "drawn from the water" (literally "pulling out"), but it was Bithiah, the Pharaoh's daughter, who named Moses (Exodus 2:10), not his mother, Jochebed. (For accuracy's sake: Bithiah's name was actually Tharmuth, according the apocryphal accounts, but most know her by this alternative name, so we will continue using it.) As a result, there is a hole in time when we don't know Moses' true Hebrew name. It would make sense, as often as the Hebrew women named their babies in relation to a circumstance at the time of birth, that Jochebed might have originally named her little one something that reflected the genocidal, baby-hiding conditions surrounding this birth. Knowing a bit of background of how the Israelites typically went about naming their children (it was most often a deeply spiritual affair, wherein the name bestowed was a sort of promissory note to or covenant between man and God), Moses' first name might have been Azariah, meaning "one whom Jehovah aids," or something to that effect. But apart from historically unverifiable traditions/legends and a few ancient, obscure, and likely unreliable commentators who proclaim to have the answer (none of which is in agreement with the other, by the way), the world will never know what moniker was originally the promise over Moses' head.

Immediately, even from this early in his tale, Mr. Misfit can't be known by his true, covenantal name—the title that would have best defined his identity to the very people he would later lead to freedom.

It's not the most poetic of beginnings, all things considered. To a Jew of his time, no Egyptian nicknames or second names given by daughters of royalty speak to the destiny of a child of Yahweh than that first title. In the case of our main character, he will only ever be known by what Bithiah—a pagan who probably wasn't led by Yahweh in her decision—casually chose as his forever identity: Mr. Drawn from the Water.

In any case, Jochebed had no choice but to place her son's fate in the hands of Jehovah, so into a waterproof basket goes our tiny misfit-in-training.

In the Beginning, God...Carried Baskets?

Okay, this is the part where at least a thousand theologians share a corporate groan. What our culture has done to the biblically accurate imagery of the beginning of the Moses story is nothing short of annihilation. Though the basket-in-the-river scene may not be the most important moment in Moses' life, considering everything that occurred from the burning bush to the delivery of the Law at Sinai, it's certainly one of the most iconic moments. We hear Moses spoken of in a sermon or teaching, and one of three pictures pops to mind. The first two are of a man holding up a staff as the sea parts and climbs into giant walls, and of that same man, long beard whipping in the wind, angrily holding aloft the stone tablets while wrath-invoked lightning strikes in the background. As far as we can tell from responsible Bible study, these concepts aren't completely off base.

The third picture, however, is of this popular theological train wreck: a baby in a basket, whooshing around on wild Nile River rapids, barely escaping the gnashing jaws of alligators as he is ruthlessly bashed against the rocks and heavy reeds. During all this thrashing about, the basket doesn't have a lid (whoopsie, bit of an oversight there, Jochebed?), so all this motion would have, by anyone's logic, thrown the three-month-old nonswimmer to his watery death no farther than ten feet into his journey. (Watch *Prince of Egypt* again sometime if you don't recall this depiction. The movie does very well in giving God much glory, and the soundtrack is simply beautiful. Nevertheless, a cartoon should never be the lens through which a scriptural passage is viewed.) Since, by some miracle, the baby in this scenario appears to miraculously survive for miles downstream to Bithiah's bathing shore, we also fill in the blanks in our imagination of an endangered Miriam. There she is, twelve or so years old at the time, running through the thickets, tripping over sticks, skinning her knee on a stone—doing the opposite of hiding quietly in close proximity to the wild predators that would have been waiting for a meal at the water's edge—as she rushes to keep an eye on the basket haphazardly carrying her brother. Then, at an abrupt dead-end of the Nile, where the former rapids inexplicably disappear and turn into a pond with lily pads, Bithiah is occupied with a relaxing, routine bath. Suddenly, a perfectly clean, brand-new, untorn basket with a happy, cooing, totally untraumatized Hebrew baby floats into view, gliding across the calm, open waters. Bithiah orders her servant to retrieve the mysterious bundle, proceeds to name the child, and then takes him in to live in the palace from that day forward; he will never see his family or people again, and he will never know that he was a Jew.

Oddly enough, that's not how it went down.

First, many miss the fact that Jochebed's choice of parting with her son via the water was a technicality that placed her in obedience to the king's command that all baby boys be "cast into the Nile River" (Exodus 1:22). This basket maneuver, commentators acknowledge, "is just within the law. She had indeed thrown her son into the river as ordered."[21] Pretty clever mother, wasn't she? Now, when Bithiah discovers the baby, Moses' fate would not solely rely on a blend of her mercy on human life and her shamelessness in disregarding her father's own law about Hebrew offspring. Instead, she would have immediately known that it was a silent petition for mercy from a Hebrew mother who had actually *obeyed* the Pharaoh, but whose son might be allowed to live due to a technicality. And don't think this is all a theory based on pure speculation. Much other evidence supports this unspoken arrangement.

For example: The bath of Bithiah wasn't a routine act of hygiene. Under normal conditions, a royal princess of the palace wouldn't have been caught dead taking a bath in the same river as the poor, common folk. This would be far beneath her as a royal, and it is certain she had the option of bathing indoors. At this time in Egypt, even regular— not royal—homes had bathtubs, if the family was wealthy enough to afford one. In fact, probably around five hundred to seven hundred years before Moses was even born, affluent Egyptians had hot tubs big enough for several people to relax in. A giant, bowl-shaped structure would be filled with water, and then stones that had been heated to the point of turning red would be lowered onto the floor of the tub, increasing the water temperature to whatever custom level of heat the group preferred. Because of the nearly-roasting climate in Egypt, these baths were more for therapeutic and medicinal purposes than social. But also because of the climate and the sandy, dusty terrain, Egyptians in general had to keep themselves clean to avoid sickness and disease. This is part of the reason hygiene was important in Egyptian culture, and why a royal would never, even for the sake of appearances, be seen cleansing her body in water shared by the poor, as well as by frogs, bugs, and other potential yuck factors. The palace would have no doubt been equipped with multiple bathing facilities, and probably with a shower, as those also existed at the time (a lower ceiling with multiple small holes would be installed in the bathhouse, and servants would poor water over the top, creating a similar sprinkling system as what we have today).

Everyone *else* might bathe in the Nile, but not a rich person…and *not* a princess.

If the scholars are correct, this "bath" was the enactment of a solemn, religious ritual. It began with the royal family (or select members) bathing in the "sacred stream." In Exodus 2:5, we read that the maidens of the princess "walked along the riverside." In proper cultural, historical, and lingual context, this doesn't describe a casual stroll, but a procession—a sort of "walking-in-a-line" sequence. The classic 1871 *Jamieson-Fausset-Brown Bible Commentary* goes on to say:

> Peculiar sacredness was attached to those portions of the Nile which flowed near the temples. The water was there fenced off as a protection from the crocodiles; and doubtless the princess had an enclosure reserved for her own use, the road to which seems to have been well known to Jochebed.[22]

In other words, the basket never could have reached Bithiah in the first place unless it was placed purposefully on the other side of the private fence leading directly to her. From technically acting within the limit of the Pharaoh's edict to strategically placing her basket within the princess' privately fenced ceremony zone, Jochebed knew very well what she was doing, and that baby was never thrashing about, Hollywood-style, over whitewater rapids.

In fact, in an oft-missed—but plainly stated—detail listed right in front of our faces, Jochebed placed Moses "in the reeds by the river's bank" (Exodus 2:3), where the water was calm and the basket would have almost immediately become entangled among river plants anyway. The spot described in this verse, scholars explain, would have been referring to "shallow water, where *the current could not carry the basket away*, with *less danger of crocodiles* than on an open sandbank or beach. There would also be some *protection from the heat of the sun*, in the reeds."[23]

Truth be told, though, it's not a "basket" we're really talking about, anyway. Scholars *do* use the word "basket" during this discussion for simplicity and to avoid stopping for frequent clarification in their writings. However, this word is actually from the Hebrew "boat," appearing only in one other biblical account, where it is translated as "ark" (in the Noah story). What Jochebed actually built her son was "a miniature Nile boat,"[24] experts say, which would have made any potential movement on the water easier and smoother than what we imagine when we think "basket in the river."

Now, does some of Moses' story look a little bit more like yours than it did fifteen minutes ago?

We have this idea that, for people like Moses, everything started off grand right from the beginning. It's all huge and miraculous and sensational and opulent. Reading the river verses the way our culture tends to interpret them is like taking an emotional journey through a barrage of thrilling, extraordinary, and romantic adventure. It's the farthest thing from "relatable." Then we look at how "regular," "mundane," "predictable," or "anticlimactic" our own stories are by comparison, and we think, *Okay, maybe Moses was a little eccentric, but I was never significant enough for God to have carried me through the rapids and past the mouths of hungry gators in a basket like that!*

But consider what we're talking about. Reimagining the scenario with all this information in mind looks much closer to this: Baby Drawn from the Water has mostly been chillin' out under the shade of the reeds in a mini boat, behind a safety fence, probably a few feet from where his mother placed him a half hour or so before she knew that the princess would start her ceremony. He's not sinking, because Jochebed has waterproofing skills (Exodus 2:3), but he's not really going anywhere either, as his boat is likely wedged between two clusters of reed stalks. If anything, the breeze that is common near watery embankments is probably causing the reeds to sway, gently rocking the three-month-old back and forth, comforting him. Miriam, far from panicked and out of breath, is sitting crisscross applesauce among the tall weeds nearby, watching calmly. She mindlessly fiddles with a stick, poking at the wet sand while she waits to see what Bithiah will do with the baby after his inevitable cries, coos, or fussing disrupts her ritual.

Yet—and this is the best part!—God's power and provision are still woven throughout this story, despite the fact that reality is a little less "bang! pow! pizazz!" as we've assumed. The theologians behind *Jamieson-Fausset-Brown* had this basket-in-the-river concept figured out 150 years ago, and they shared our sentiment about God's undeniable presence in the story quite vividly—all while acknowledging that the romance is still overwhelmingly present:

> The narrative is picturesque. No tale of romance ever described a plot more skillfully laid or more full of interest in the development. The...ark [basket], the slime and pitch, the choice of the time and place...the stationing of the sister as a watch of the proceedings, her timely suggestion of a nurse, and the engagement of the mother herself—all bespeak a more than ordinary measure of ingenuity as well as intense solicitude on the part of the parents. But the origin of the scheme was most probably owing to a divine suggestion, as its success was due to an over-ruling Providence, who...preserved the child's life.... Hence it is said to have been done by faith (Heb 11:23), either in the general promise of deliverance, or some special revelation made to Amram and Jochebed—and in this view, the pious couple gave a beautiful example of a firm reliance on the word of God, united with an active use of the most suitable means.[25]

Just because the truth isn't accompanied by trumpet blasts and shooting stars doesn't make it a lesser truth. When a true story involves an act of divine intervention—a supernatural intrusion of the hand of God that redirects circumstances and inspires people to move along the path He paves toward optimal endings—that doesn't go away just because the story is less sensational than the movie. *God* made Moses, *God* led Jochebed to devise a plan, and then *God* ensured the successful delivery of that baby boy into the hands of a woman who was likely the only one who could have saved him the way she did.

This is the same Almighty who made *you*.

The next time you're tempted to say, "My story started off a bit rocky and dysfunctional," remember that you might have more in common with Moses than you thought. And it doesn't stop there. Let's see what happens next, beginning at Exodus 2:7.

Dude...Who *Are* You?

After Miriam witnesses the princess' compassionate expression, she slips from her hiding place and offers to retrieve a wet nurse from the Hebrew women, a plan that Bithiah finds agreeable. Jochebed responds to the call and takes the baby home with her until his weaning year, which in that day was somewhere around four to five years old. This timing is in line with what we know of ancient Egyptian customs. It might be surprising to some of us today who would consider a kindergartner too old to still be breastfeeding, or to those who know the DreamWorks Animation *Prince of Egypt* version of the Moses story, but history acknowledges this as common in many ancient cultures, as well as in the case of adoption. Mesopotamian adoption documents speak of the "foundling infants" who, for the baby's best chance at survival in vulnerable periods, were left to live with a wet nurse and encouraged to suckle at the breast for as long as possible.[26] Only then would an official adoption be carried out. This is what technically takes place in Exodus 2:10, after the boy did some growing up already, as the beginning of the verse states:

> And the child grew, and she brought him unto Pharaoh's daughter, and he became her son. And she called his name Moses: and she said, "Because I drew him out of the water."

At this part in the story, for the first time, Moses is assigned a name that the reader is privy to, and this is also when Moses begins to live in the palace.

Part 2: The Floating Misfit

Prior to this, the boy's entire identity—up to and around age five—has been spent as a Hebrew getting to know his siblings, his parents, and his God. Jochebed not only got to remain united with her boy, she was even paid wages for her "services" as a wet nurse (Exodus 2:9). The question then becomes: Did Moses know he was a Hebrew? Or was he taken to the palace and raised as a high-ranking member of Egyptian society, flippantly ignoring the woes of his people? Did he, like in the movies and cartoons, stumble upon the cryptic hieroglyphs of some distant passageway at night with a torch—it's the movies; you have to put the dramatic torch in there—discovering once and for all his true identity? Then, did this lead to his subsequent yet inevitable mental breakdown that resulted in his taking an Egyptian slave driver's life?

Even the most responsible Bible study doesn't answer all the questions we have about the approximate thirty-five year span between Bithiah's adoption of Moses and the slave driver's death (Moses is forty when he murders; cf. Acts 7:23). First of all, there is almost no dismissing Acts 7:25, which reads without ambiguity that "[Moses] supposed his brethren would have understood how that God by his hand would deliver them: but they understood not." This verse is wedged between the murder (that's what we're calling it for now, but keep reading) of the Egyptian and the confrontation by the angry Hebrew, whose words directly led to Moses' flight from Egypt. Thus, the timing pretty much forces the idea that by the age of forty, Moses already knew he was: a) a Jew, and b) the deliverer of Israel. Additionally, Hebrews 11:24–27 clearly states that, "By faith, Moses, when he was come to years" (meaning also at this moment in time), his motive in leaving Egypt was (at least in part) to join his people, the Israelites, suffer in their affliction, forsake his former life of riches, and fear God more than he does the Pharaoh.

However, because of the lack of narrative describing what took place during the palace years, the discussion has been put out there for theologians and exegetes to consider for millennia just *how much* Moses knew, and when. (However, we would like to point out that it's unrealistic to assume that he grew up a pompous prince, uncaring for the slaves outside, then killed an Egyptian and suddenly [and conveniently] fell under the conviction to join his people. Again, more on this to come.) No matter how clear it might seem already, academics (and Hollywood producers) keep resurrecting the idea that Moses had no idea who he was, or raising the question of whether he knew he was poised as deliverer, and so on. Sometimes, during speculative moments like these, we can read what the Bible says and also consider what it does not say. Remember that this is Moses' story, and he is credited as being the author of Exodus. It's *his* story that he's personally documenting, and by the time we arrive at the very next verse in order, Exodus 2:11, Moses, in his autobiographical admission, identifies the slaves as his "brethren." If he hadn't known he was a Hebrew, if this had been kept a secret while he was brought up as an Egyptian who "only coincidently had the same features and skin color as the slaves outside," Moses would have had reason to document that relevant detail. It can't be proven that he would have written that part, but it's certainly logical. Many of these research materials about Moses generally agree that it's the absence of any mention of concealed identity that best argues for the probability that Moses always knew who he was and where he came from.

In addition, scholars acknowledge that Moses spent enough time with his mother at home amidst the Hebrews and their culture during his early developmental years that it would likely be impossible for him to forget those memories completely. It even says in the book of Jubilees (47:9) that his dad had begun to educate him: "Amram thy father taught thee writing."

It's nearly certain that, despite his youth, the conviction of the Hebrews around Moses was such that he would have had received as much education about Yahweh as his community could have pressed into his mind before he was turned over to be raised by the pagans. It's also extremely likely that, as conversations took place with or around

Moses leading up to the moment he would be placed in palace care, folks may have discussed whether his princely rearing was a part of God's plan to free the Israelites. In other words, it's possible that four- or five-year-old Moses not only knew all along that he was a Hebrew, but he also might have been groomed to some extent by loved ones to believe that his role in the palace would be the very tool by which the royal family would someday be challenged.

And why not? Sure, it's only speculation (and we wouldn't go making that into a movie or cartoon that further perpetuates erroneous concepts about Moses), but since we're "bringing him to life on the pages" a bit right now, let's go there.

King Evil says all boy babies die, and *this one* lives against all the odds. As sure as he's alive, he's back home, legally and under the sanction of the princess, herself, so nobody can stop Moses' family from investing in him spiritually. As soon as he's weaned, he will be handed over to royalty and raised as a prince over all of Egypt. As he grows, he will be interacting with, *and possibly influencing*, future authorities whose throne will one day determine the fate of the Jews. With this scenario as a backdrop, why on earth wouldn't the Hebrews—or the whole nation of Israel, for that matter—be instilling into Moses the pride of his people and preparing him for one day intervening for them?

It's food for thought, anyway.

The bottom line is that the Bible doesn't say that Moses grew up in the dark regarding his relatives, but it does say that he recognized them as "brethren" even before the murder. So, for a moment, assuming his awareness, take a moment to imagine how much a misfit he would have thought himself to be:

- *He's not an Egyptian.* Not really. Not by birth, anyway, which undoubtedly has its challenges in the palace. He's going to look different from the others in the royal family and, these authors are certain, he will be treated differently than the others as well. Outside the palace, amidst his true family, he might be the embodiment of a hope glimmer, a tiny hero in training that twelve full tribes prayed for on the daily, a giant duck in the small and humble slave pond…but he would not live with that support in his home. Inside the palace, we believe, there were those in his company who wouldn't have appreciated a prince born from Hebrew blood and roots. Moses probably felt some level of racial tension as he grew. Like a small duck in a wilderness-of-riches pond—he knew deep down he didn't actually belong. How far that tension reached and its emotional effects on Moses is anyone's guess, but it was probably present to some degree all the time—even if that was only manifest in Moses' self-consciousness and not in any direct abuse, neglect, or disdain by the royals.

- *He's not a Hebrew.* Again, not really. He may have been born of a Hebrew mother and father, but where it counts, he will never be able to say that he truly, deeply knows what it means to be one of his own. His privileged surroundings sowed a "seed of disconnect" between himself and the heart cries of his oppressed relatives. The world of whippings, lashings, beatings, hard labor, dehydrated bodies under the sun, festering wounds, weakness, disease, and filth, *all* of that was outside—where "the slaves" lived. And he wasn't one of them. Nor could he have sincerely enjoyed his individual liberty from that world. Though he wouldn't come to full understanding of the extent of the Hebrews' suffering until later (Exodus 2:11), his entire life, every time Moses heard a distant whip crack, or saw a newly built wall, he was reminded that it was his brothers and sisters out there. Each grand, opulent meal he enjoyed in the palace—amidst countless servants who would tend to Prince Moses' every desire—stood in sharp contrast to the humble dinner upon the Jewish table… a table that also might be entirely bare at any given time. No doubt, Moses cared. The later death of an Egyptian slave driver by Moses' hands is enough proof that he cared enough to defend the Jews, proof that he wasn't calloused or aloof to his peoples' hardships. His position in the palace and his faith in Yahweh introduced a nagging guilt that lingered and hovered constantly, robbing him of the ability to relish in luxury while *his people* made bricks (cf. Hebrews 11:24–27).

Therein lies the problem: Both the Egyptians *and* the Hebrews were "his people," but Moses wasn't truly "one of" either of them.

He wasn't an Egyptian, but he wasn't a Hebrew.

He wasn't a prince, but he wasn't a slave.

So, what *was* he?

He was a misfit. And he felt it.

Moses didn't "belong" for the first forty years of his life. And though the Word is silent on how he felt and what he thought during his first thirty-five year period, we can imagine that Moses had his fair share of loner moments. His misfit rap sheet was there from birth when he wasn't supposed to be born. Then, it was carried into the palace where he was the illegitimate prince of slaves. And somewhere between his early years and the day he murdered an Egyptian soldier, his speech impediment developed.

He Doesn't "Word Good"

Oh, wait…didn't you know? Moses had a speech impediment. Yeah. The deliverer of Israel, the man who challenged the Pharaoh and won, the leader of an entire nation through whom the very Law and Ten Commandments of God were spoken—God's über mouthpiece—couldn't talk. Well, not without extreme difficulty, anyway. God chose a man with a speech difficulty to be His lead spokesperson.

Though this disability isn't brought up in the story until later, when Moses was arguing with God about speaking to the Pharaoh (Exodus 4:10; 6:12, 30), we are choosing to include it here because, if we are correct, Moses' condition would have started as a young child or teen, but it would have caused embarrassment and social issues in crucial developmental years for a young adult or fully grown man. That's right about here-ish in the narrative. We don't know for certain how his disability would have affected his relationships—especially his years growing up in the palace where he may or may not have been forced to do much talking anyway and, as royalty, he wouldn't have been heckled by the general public for it.

What we do know is that this condition was such a stumbling block for Moses that he continuously referred to it as a reason he wasn't worthy to be speaking on God's behalf. In Exodus 4:10, his words, "I am slow of speech, and of a slow tongue," appear to imply that his main problem was related to the literal utterance of language because of his mouth being too "slow" to do what God is asking. However, his next couple of protests were a little more colorful, as he used language associated with covenantal concepts, such as saying he had "uncircumcised lips." Though this latter reference might make a reader of a more modern translation raise an eyebrow, the Hebrew words here (*arel sapa*) literally do mean "uncircumcised lips." But, obviously, since a literal circumcision of "lips" is absurd, Moses certainly intended the reference as a metaphor for something else. A metaphor for *what* is the question.

But hold on! Doesn't Acts 7:22 say that Moses was "mighty in words and deeds"?

Yes, but don't misunderstand. The emphasis here doesn't have to be upon Moses' ability to articulate, but upon the weight his words had—however they sounded coming out of his mouth—upon the eventual fate of the Pharaoh and the rest of Egypt. *Barnes' Notes on the Whole Bible* explains:

In *words*—From Exodus 4:10, it seems that Moses was "slow of speech, and of a slow tongue." When it is said that he was mighty in words, it means that he was mighty in his communications to Pharaoh, though they were spoken by his brother Aaron. Aaron was in his place, and "Moses" addressed Pharaoh through him, who was appointed to deliver the message, Exodus 4:11–16.[27]

It's also important to remember that Moses' in-person speech may not even be what is referenced here in Acts. Not all words have to be spoken if words on scrolls can also be powerful, if they were written down and passed down to countless generations of Jews (which they were)... who therefore followed his "mighty instructions" (Mosaic Law). *Jamieson-Fausset-Brown* states: "**mighty in words**—Though defective in utterance (Ex 4:10); his *recorded speeches* fully bear out what is here said."[28]

The discussion among scholars about Moses' speech problem has been carried on for thousands of years—well, since the time of Moses. And we mean that literally. Moses' authorship of the first five books in the Bible was only barely finished when the skill of scriptural interpretation began with the rabbis. Therefore, we aren't going to be able to do the topic the justice it deserves here and now by providing the lengthy examination.

As for the shorter breakdown, just to get a little bearing on the conclusion we're leading to, we'll quickly address whether this "speech" problem could have been spiritual or mental rather than a condition of the literal mouth or tongue.

First, many of the theories that the references were only symbolic, as opposed to involving physiology, are problematic. For instance, one popular argument relies on the fact that the Hebrew description of "heavy" language in Exodus 4:10 was synonymous with "deep" language, meaning that Moses was especially profound. These scholars have no problem explaining why, in Hebrew, one word is synonymous with another, and it could actually mean "profound." But the logic dies here: Why, if Moses was "so deep" and "so profound," would he use his excellent communication traits to claim he wasn't a good communicator, when these characteristics are in fact benchmarks of a great communicator? The logic cancels itself out. Imagine this in modern words: "No, God, don't use *me* to speak to the Pharaoh! I can't speak because I'm just so good at it!"

Some in this camp say that Moses' deep, profound thoughts actually affected his ability to isolate a single idea fast enough to articulate it—a "mind-is-faster-than-the-mouth" conundrum—and that his speech was therefore paralyzed or slowed while he struggled knowing which "heavy" thing on his mind to address first. But this take on it is challenged as well, in part because of Moses' complaint that he was "not eloquent" (which is a matter of lacking smoothness, elegance, and persuasion in one's spoken words, not a matter of trying to articulate thought *into* spoken words).

Moving to another theory, there's a linguistics argument that suggests Moses was fluent in Egyptian (pre-Coptic), as this was the language spoken at the palace, but that he didn't know the Hebrew language of his people, and therefore couldn't smoothly intermediate between both sides. Or, if we reverse that—theorizing that he was fluent in Hebrew but couldn't speak to the Pharaoh due to a language barrier—we arrive at another theory. Both of these are nearly impossible. One casts an irrational (and unnecessary) "silent era" onto his palace years; the other assumes he only barely communicated with his wife and father-in-law for the forty years he lived in the desert with Israelites.

Still others explain that the association between circumcision and cleanliness ties Moses' insecurity to a matter of spiritual imperfection or unpreparedness. This is a possibility linguistically, but the context keeps hitting a snag. Of all the "purely symbolism" explanations, this "spiritually imperfect/unprepared" approach might have been the most convincing to us if it didn't require further explanation as to why, in Exodus 4:10, he talked about the slowness of literal speech, not a hesitation sparked by being emotionally or spiritually immature or unprepared. Last of all, because an instance of "uncircumcised ears" appears later in Jeremiah 6:10, some of these symbols are tossed out the window because the euphemism might work with "lips," but not with "ears," and so on. After a while, it just gets too complicated to even be practical that Moses, in two words, meant to insinuate all these intricate spiritual truths.

In fact, after a while, most theories about Moses' speech problem require intricate, unnecessary, and laboring steps to "the deeper meaning" or "the other explanation," when a literal impediment is such a readily available, perfectly fitting possibility. (This is true immediately in Exodus 4:10. It's also true for 6:12 and 6:30 of that book, though not as immediately. For reasons that would require us to stop here and look closely at all the spiritual significance behind the act of circumcision, as well as the actual act of circumcision, itself, we will skip visiting at length why, but suffice it to say that we believe Moses' circumcision metaphor was a symbol, but it was a one of a literal impediment.)

As to what kind of an impediment Moses had, there are a few possibilities. An orofacial myofunctional disorder is when the bones and muscles in the face grow abnormally, causing a dysfunction not only in speech, but also frequently in eating, drinking, and breathing through the nose. It could be this, but since none of these other difficulties were mentioned in Scripture, it's anyone's guess. A disorder called dysarthria is less likely, because it requires a right-hemisphere brain injury to weaken the muscles of the face and jaw (this is what happens to cause the slurred speech of a stroke victim, for example). This, too, assumes that Moses would have left his brain injury out of his autobiographical/biblical accounts. With this same shadow of doubt, many other injury-related speech problems can also be only marginally considered. (One clearly unbelievable legend that can probably be attributed to Jewish scholar and commentator Bahye ben Asher [also known as Rabbeinu Bahye] around the turn of the fourteenth century starts with the claim that a very young Moses wouldn't stop trying to grab at the flashy crown of the Pharaoh. Pharaoh's men told him this was a bad omen, so the child would have to be killed. Instead, however, Moses would be tested. A golden bowl was brought in and presented to Moses next to a pile of glowing coal. An angel guided Moses' hand to grab the coal, after which the young Moses placed his fingers in his mouth to suck the sting of the burn, yet his fingers were so burned that they afflicted his tongue permanently, rendering him physically incapable of sounding palatal consonants such as the letters *s* and *t*. We don't know if Bahye invented this idea, or if he merely perpetuated it, but uhhh...no. That's not what happened.

However, at the end of the day, the actual issue of "slow speech" that Moses appeared to be describing in this original conversation with God was most likely a bad stutter. That fits the literal "slow speech," "slow tongue" lamentation; it doesn't clash with reasonable interpretations of the "uncircumcised lips" reference; and the symptoms of the condition can agree with the biblical account. The celebrated theological and unrivalled master of multiple ancient biblical languages, Dr. Michael Heiser, agrees: "[Moses] says, 'I can't talk well.' And it is true that you could look at those Hebrew terms there and it could be that Moses was a stutterer. That's certainly possible."[29]

And there it is, folks. A stutter. Moses, himself, the soon-to-be leader of the nation of God, all the chosen people, all the souls looking to him for guidance and direction through the Exodus, through the parted waters, past endless deserts with fiery pillars and clouds leading them all over the place, through the wilderness and around mountains for forty years...all this leadership from a man who didn't believe he could string a sentence together.

Heiser is one of thousands of scholars who acknowledges the stutter probability. In Heiser's case, though, he goes on to explain why none of this matters, because the point is not whether Moses had a stutter; it's about trusting that God will carry the words, and it's about not making excuses (Moses had plenty in these passages) when we've been given direction from God.

In a different book, we would agree with Heiser that the stutter is a marginal issue. That the bottom line is: Don't argue with God. Don't make excuses. Don't tell God why He was wrong when he picked you. Just do what God is saying.

However, in *this* book, the speech impediment matters.

That's because the guy has been called by God—*the Almighty Creator of all of the universe*—to perform leadership in a way that diametrically counters his flawed capabilities! This is the Lord God, King of all Heaven, choosing a stuttering Hebrew who wasn't really born into royalty to lead his people like a king…even though he cannot speak!

He. Is. A. *Misfit*!

God could have chosen any human on the planet, and He chose the one who is nearly mute!

Why?

Hmmm. Dunno. Just out of "mere speculation," though, could it be because He likes to confound those humans who think they're all that and a bag of beef tacos by using a humble vessel they would never expect to carry out His power and will (cf. 1 Corinthians 1:27)?

Naw, naw. It couldn't be that. Sorry. We got excited for a second.

Oh hang on, we've got another one. Maybe it's because God's power is made even *better* and *stronger* through us when we are weak and rely on Him to do wonders through us (cf. 2 Corinthians 12:9–11)?

Mmmm…probably not.

Oh, oh, oh! Is it because He, Himself, can help us with our flaws, teach us what to say in scary situations and things like that, because He's the Designer who made us in the first place and has the final word over whether our misfit imperfections are going to keep us from doing what He's asked us to do (Exodus 4:11–12; Luke 12:12)?

What are we thinking? Where are we coming up with these ideas, anyway?

Excuse our sarcastic, hyperbolic tones. It's *far* too often that Christians, especially misfits, say God can't use them for a specific job because of X, when X is exactly *why* God has chosen them for that specific job. Nowhere has this ever been more radically true than with Moses, who doubted his ability to speak, then went down in history as one of the most important speakers since Creation.

Now, where were we…?

God's "Thou Shalt Not Kill" Messenger Just, Uhhh, Killed a Guy

Let's go back to Exodus 2:11. Moses is all grown up at the age of forty, and he's well educated in "all the wisdom of the Egyptians" (Acts 7:22–23). Although the Bible doesn't explicitly say so, a running assumption for many scholars and theologians is that Moses had the same upbringing and training in the Pharaoh's court as any of his princelings, making him 100 percent equal as a potential future Pharaoh. Whether the Egyptian leaders would have given him the opportunity to take the throne or not—based not only on his wisdom, education, and governing skills but also on how the culture felt about his being a Jew by blood—is not recorded. Also, we remain completely in the dark regarding what the Hebrew slaves were hoping and praying for or expecting God to do with Moses on their behalf. For this reason, many academics have attempted (and some impressively so) to fill in the blanks. One possible scenario involves the idea that the Hebrews believed God saved Moses specifically so he would *become* the next Pharaoh.

That politics in that region and time would have allowed a Hebrew to rule as king of the Egyptians doesn't appear to be too hard to believe, considering that Joseph, another Hebrew, had already arisen as viceroy (second only to the Pharaoh in power) about one to three centuries earlier. However, since this took place centuries after Joseph was prominent in the land, it could be that all the current Egyptians had only ever thought of foreigners as worthy of being slaves while one lucky one was adopted into the palace, and maybe a Hebrew Pharaoh wasn't as likely. (Also note that there isn't any proof supporting the idea that the crown would descend through a daughter [Bithiah] of the Pharaoh before it would a son, which is a consideration for the ancient world that makes Moses' connection to the crown less likely as well.) But "likely" is not the box that the God of the Israelites lived in, so nothing political really mattered. It's probable, all things considered, that the Hebrews saw the adoption of Moses by Bithiah as the beginning of their promise of deliverance, and that this would come to them through Moses as Pharaoh (or at least as advisor just under him). At this point in the story, he's forty years old, and we don't know how much talk is occurring behind closed doors of the palace regarding whether this Israelite will be promoted soon, or how far up the ladder that promotion might reach.

What we do know is that he is filthy rich, extremely powerful, well-educated, highly cultured, and is walking tall when a sudden tragedy occurs.

This next part is stated in Scripture so quickly that it creates many questions. However, it's a turning point for Moses, so we will take a minute to consider what's actually happening. Let's look at it in Exodus, as remembered and documented by Moses, and in Acts, as reiterated by Stephen in his bold address to the council that led to his stoning and the diaspora of the New Covenant Jews:

> And it came to pass in those days, when Moses was grown, that he went out unto his brethren, and looked on their burdens: and he spied an Egyptian smiting an Hebrew, one of his brethren. And he looked this way and that way, and when he saw that there was no man, he slew the Egyptian, and hid him in the sand. (Exodus 2:11–12)

And when he was full forty years old, it came into his heart to visit his brethren the children of Israel. And seeing one of them suffer wrong, he defended him, and avenged him that was oppressed, and smote the Egyptian: For he supposed his brethren would have understood how that God by his hand would deliver them: but they understood not. (Acts 7:23–25)

Let's look at these last two verses again in the ESV (a modern translation these authors deem very reliable):

And seeing one of them being wronged, he defended the oppressed man and avenged him by striking down the Egyptian. He supposed that his brothers would understand that God was giving them salvation by his hand, but they did not understand.

Right away, the motive is clear: Moses thought, when he was spotted killing a violent slave driver, that his people would know he was motivated by the responsibility of defending and freeing them from oppression. To reiterate: He thought it was obvious that this was his duty, and he believed the people would've known that by now. Moses' nature, according to everything in the language of the narrative up to this point, was not one of a murderer. In fact, Numbers 12:3 declares that, more than every other man upon the earth, he was known to be "meek" (gentle). We needn't look further or deeper than this to see that Moses' motive was not born out of anything devious, wicked, or vengeful. Discussions of premeditation are irrelevant, since he had stumbled upon the scene just seconds before he reacted. Today's court lingo has a number of death-related terms swirling through our minds—"murder," "manslaughter," "homicide," "first degree," "second degree," "felony," and "capital"—some of which have been historically applied to Moses because of the accusation in verse 14 (we're getting to that).

Was the act, itself, the right thing to do? Certainly some scholars have taken that position, defending Moses and believing that even the death of the Egyptian was a part of God's plan (in part because that led to Moses fleeing to Midian for the next forty years of spiritual training). Others say that Moses' heart was in the right place, but that he acted impulsively; therefore, the Egyptian's death would not have been a part of God's initial plan, though He was able to use Moses' mistake for His purposes. Still others call this a "murder," believing that, although Moses was eventually rehabilitated and redeemed, he was guilty of a rage kill. But as highly debated as this moment is in Moses' life for modern scholars, and for as clear as his "deliverer" motive is in Scripture, we're still left with a dramatic misfit-ism: Moses, by the time he would become known as the one who brought down the Ten Commandments with "Thou shalt not kill" right there on the tablets, will have already been known as the one who killed a man. Come on. Is that God using His anointed, got-it-together, textbook-perfection superhero? Or is that the picture of a misfit stumbling through, trying to figure out how to even carry out what God has asked?

As mentioned earlier, this account in Acts seems clear that Moses acted in righteous defense of his brethren. But, if that were true, why did he look both ways before he killed the guy, buried the body in the sand, and then freaked out and fled the territory when he knew he was going to get caught (Exodus 2:13–15)?

There appears to be a wrinkle on the page here. Let's iron it out.

As a quick disclaimer, we're not against admitting that Moses or any other Bible character may be guilty of murder. We've been referring to it up to this point as "murder," and we have no problem acknowledging biblical misfits who have committed crimes of this magnitude and are still used by God. In fact, David's guilt in the story of Bathsheba and Uriah was worse, because it involved a lengthy season of premeditation. We all know that God punished David for his crimes. Yet, don't we also know that it wasn't the end of David's story and of his usefulness to God? Similarly, if Moses murdered a man, then he did, and we don't have any reservations in allowing for that possibility. But Moses' "misfit" traits are frequently tied to this event, and in this book, we believe it's important to break that down just a little so we can see into and feel the real man.

Rewinding the story to just before it happened, many details about the hours leading up to this incident aren't clear. For instance: Had Moses gotten out and about among his people before this moment? Commentator Albert Barnes was pretty confident in his assessment:

> The Egyptian princess had not concealed from him the fact of his belonging to the oppressed race, nor is it likely that she had debarred him from contact with his...mother and her family, whether or not she became aware of the true relationship.[30]

If Barnes' take is accurate, Moses might have visited his family and friends many times. (This theory is also supported by the fact that Moses went out to visit them two days in a row in this passage.) Somehow, though he most likely had some exposure to the oppression of Israel, he hadn't ever been fully informed of its dramatic extent before now. (Maybe the Hebrews would have acted as if they were in the presence of royalty and restrained themselves from bum rushing Moses with their woes? We don't know. We only know that it's probable that he had some regular interaction with his people prior to this day, and that he didn't know just how bad their situation was.)

On this occasion, something happens that shows him the magnitude of the Hebrews' oppression, as is captured by the vague string of words, "and looked on their burdens." Some scholars say that this wording suggests a specific and intentional assessment of his people, whether he had visited casually before or not. This is the stance of *Jamieson-Fausset-Brown*:

> [Moses] purposed to make a full and systematic inspection of their condition in the various parts of the country where they

were dispersed…and he adopted this proceeding in pursuance of the patriotic purpose that the faith which is of the operation of God was even then forming in his heart.[31]

Others have a simpler position, interpreting "looked on their burdens" to mean that he was out for a stroll when he inadvertently happened to see something he hadn't seen before, and it affected him internally. "This phrase means more than 'to see,'" one commentary states. "It means 'to see with emotion.'"[32]

Whatever this moment in Scripture is describing, Moses fully comprehends for the first time what his brothers and sisters of God are faced with, then he sees the Egyptian in the act of killing one of his brethren with a weapon that was probably one of the standard taskmasters' "long heavy scourges, made of a tough pliant wood imported from Syria."[33] These two major shocks plainly cause Moses to snap and intervene, and the result is the death of one of Pharaoh's soldiers. But, might there be a clue in the original language as to whether we should refer to this as "murder"?

The Hebrew term *naka* appears several times in a row, in Exodus 2:11, 2:13, and 2:13. In 2:11, it's translated as "smiting"; in 2:12, "slew"; and "smitest" in 2:13 (all from KJV). Any of these instances could refer not only to killing, but also to striking or beating someone—cruel, perhaps, but not necessarily grammatically married to the premeditated intent to snuff out a life. Probably the most damning evidence that this is a murder and not an accident is what one man says to Moses the next day when Moses intervenes in a fight between two Hebrew men.

The day after he kills the slave driver, Moses is apparently out among the Hebrews, and he happens upon a physical altercation. "Wherefore smitest thou thy fellow?" Moses says, which can be reworded today to say, "Why are you beating up your friend?" The one who started the fight responds, "Who made thee a prince and a judge over us? intendest thou to kill me, as thou killedst the Egyptian?" (Exodus 2:13–14).

Right here, in Scripture, in text that is supposed to be infallible, Moses is accused of "murder." The Hebrew *harag*—here translated as "kill" and "killedst"—means "to murder," and, well, that's pretty clear, isn't it?

But remember that this is not the text itself, the voice of God as Author, directly communicating to the reader that "murder" or "homicide" is what Moses is guilty of. It's the text reporting one character's accusation of another. If a Bible character were to say to another, "You're ugly and your mama dresses you funny," then the principle of the infallibility of Scripture requires that we believe the first person did say that to the other, just as reported. We are *not*, however, required to believe that the second person is, in fact, ugly and that his mother dresses him funny. Similarly, though an angry Hebrew man accuses Moses of murder, "murder" is not the verb that appears in the story prior, when the Narrator's voice, the Author's voice, *was* explaining the events directly to the reader. As far as what the text of the Word does directly tell the reader regarding Moses' guilt, it's worthy of note that it uses *naka*—leaving the window open for interpreting all of this as an accident—instead of the less ambiguous *harag*.

In simpler terms, it could be that the Bible describes the following scenario: Moses has no intent to hurt anyone, and only wants to rescue. He runs into the scene and initially strikes a man in a righteous, noble act of defending his brethren, and, though the outcome is unintentional, the Egyptian dies. Then, Moses is unfairly accused of murder by a disgruntled Hebrew (who probably isn't impressed by the resident deliverer because he hasn't yet risen up to lead the Israelites to freedom, *or* because he's jaded by the fact that Moses would question him about beating up a man after killing one himself the previous day). This is a fair reading of Scripture, and largely has the most support in the academic world.

As to why Moses looked both ways first, only in the most modern translations do we read, "Moses looked around to make sure nobody was watching him" or, "Moses first made sure there were no witnesses." In the Hebrew, the literal translation is that Moses "turned thus thus, saw that no man, smite Egyptian," or, Moses "turned thus and thus and saw no man, so he slew the Egyptian" (Exodus 2:12). The fact that his looking both ways is even involved in the modern translations is a grievance. (One curious thought that garners almost no coverage in the academic world is why it can't be interpreted as, "Moses looked around to see if anyone else was present *who might intervene*, and seeing that there was no man around who would, he killed the Egyptian in defense of his fellow Jew." Despite this being a reasonable possibility in our opinion, not enough scholarly voices have addressed this interpretation to validate it here.) Antique commentaries are fairly unanimous in their assessment that Moses wasn't looking around to make sure there were no witnesses. Puritan theologian and commentator Matthew Poole said that Moses' glance back and forth was "not from conscience of guilt in what he intended, but from human and warrantable prudence."[34] In other words, he was just being careful before he rushed in, and no further analysis is necessary. Poole's faithful take on the entire murder incident is that this level of intervention was Moses' right, as it was his "divine and special vocation to be the ruler and deliverer of Israel," and that this death wasn't even meant to be a secret in the first place, but instead was "a signal to make it evident to the people" that he was aware of this calling.[35] In response to why Moses was described as being afraid when he found out he had been seen, Poole (and most others) believe the nervousness is linked to his punishment should the Pharaoh find out, not in any shame over having committed a perceived criminal act.[36]

Gill's Exposition takes a view similar to Poole's, insisting that Moses' looking around "did not arise from any consciousness of any evil he was about to commit, but for his own preservation, lest if seen he should be accused to Pharaoh, and suffer for it."[37] In other words, Moses believed that some higher moral law excused him of guilt, while he also knew that the law of the land (perhaps Hammurabi's Code, addressed in a bit) did not.

If this is the correct analysis, then Moses looked side to side to make sure there weren't any witnesses, because he knew what he was about to do was considered murder on a purely secular level, though he felt no conviction about whether he had done right or wrong in the eyes of God as Israel's deliverer. He then buried the body so he wouldn't have to answer to a secular authority when he was, in his heart, acting on a justifiably higher moral authority. Assuming the body wasn't found or the death wasn't witnessed, Moses could secretly claim he had defended a Hebrew, as was his "vocation," and nobody would be any the wiser. Now, he could sit and wait (still…) to be in line for the throne from which he would free his people. But later, when he was found out, he began to fear that he would have to answer to the secular authorities… and he had a lot to lose if Pharaoh then took his life, including having to answer for why God's prized deliverer was executed before any deliverance took place. This would make any normal man, no matter how emotionally strong, worry to the point of fleeing the land; it wasn't just capital punishment that he feared, but the realization that the justice he dealt the Egyptian backfired because it was enacted prematurely (or somehow out of the timing or method God planned). As such, he would not only answer to God for the deliverance he failed to bring to the people, he would answer to his people as well! Yeah…he was absolutely going to "fear" and say, "Oh no…surely they know about my deed!" whether his deed felt morally wrong to him or not.

So there you have it: the most likely (and widest accepted) explanation of Moses' "murder" charge. But before we move on, we want to show you one last important (and fascinating!) thought.

Although the "life for a life" law (Exodus 21:24) hadn't yet been recorded, the starkly similar law from the Code of Hammurabi was in effect and had an extreme degree of influence over the Egyptian culture for about two centuries prior. Moses no doubt was familiar with the idea that his life was forfeited if he was ever to be found guilty of murdering another Egyptian, and, for reasons just addressed, he wouldn't have been inclined to put that to the test frivolously. This is enough to explain any potential "guilty maneuvers" or "suspicious activity." But still, was this mere internal conviction? Or was another pre-Mosaic Law that bound the Hebrews to certain, absolute, and tangible moral regulation?

That depends. How much do you believe in Talmudic traditions?

For those who aren't familiar with some of these Jewish terms, the Mishnah is the Jewish "compendium, largely legal, containing regulations and beliefs foundational of rabbinic Judaism and thus of all later Jewish thought."[38] This is the early collection of the "Oral Tradition" or the "Oral Torah" that served as a companion to the Torah (the first five books of the Hebrew Bible—same as ours—Genesis, Exodus, Leviticus, Numbers, and Deuteronomy). The Talmud is sort of what commentaries are to us in the Christian world, except instead of focusing on the sixty-six canonical books of the Holy Bible as we know it, it's a commentary of what is stated in the Mishnah.

According to Talmudic tradition, well before Moses was born, the "Noahide Law" was given to Noah by God in an act of divine intervention around the time of the Flood to ensure that there would be *some* basis of morality to govern the hearts of men for the soon-to-be repopulated human race. These laws are:

- Do not murder.
- Do not steal.
- Do not worship false gods.
- Do not practice sexual immorality.
- Do not eat the limb of an animal before it is killed.
- Do not curse God.
- Establish courts and brings offenders to justice.[39]

As it is believed that these laws were given to Noah (and Adam before him), they are binding upon all humanity. Influenced by these laws, the writers of the Talmud acknowledge that "Do not murder" doesn't sufficiently outline what must be done in the case of an accidental death or an act of self-defense, so those issues were addressed as well, and often appear nearly identical to the situations outlined in the Mosaic Law. However, going a step further, we stumble upon a *rodef*, a late-Hebrew word with roots in Aramaic, describing a person who is in pursuit of another person with intent to murder.[40] In other words, a person in the act of killing an innocent, but who has not yet succeeded—like the Egyptian slave driver in our story.

Jewish law in this case doesn't just deal with self-defense. It states that if a *rodef* is carrying out a murder and a friend or bystander happens to witness it and intervene, just like Moses, he is exempt from punishment, even if the *rodef* dies in the process of defense. But actually, the Talmudic instruction doesn't simply end there. According to the Babylonian Talmud, in the "Sanhedrin" section, subsection 72a–73a, a person in Moses' position is *obligated* to save the innocent, even to the death of the *rodef*, if such a thing proves necessary. In other words, Moses would have been found guilty of criminal negligence if he had stood by and done nothing for his Hebrew brother. This would be a tricky situation, because the Egyptian was within his legal right to punish the slave, even unto death, while Moses was only protected by the law *of* the slaves— which would have required utmost adherence and obedience *as unto God*, while it didn't dictate anything as far as Pharaoh was concerned. If this is the position Moses was placed in, then he wouldn't have had a choice but to rescue and flee, just as he did.

So the question then becomes whether the Talmudic traditions, tracing back to Adam, are acceptable enough to exempt Moses from a "murder" charge according to the higher moral law of God. One argument against it is that many traditions could be synonymously titled "legends," with origin stories that are simply unverifiable. There is never going to be any solid, irrefutable proof to back it up.

One argument for this Noahide Law tradition, however, is that something—be it through Adam, Noah, or someone else—existed before that time that communicated to Israel at least the very basics of moral standards and how to recognize sin. We believe this because, at this point in the Bible (and even well before tracing back to Adam), there is an attitude of recognition of at least a fundamental law or moral code. The acknowledgment of "sin" is proof enough that a set of rules exists to keep that sin accountable—i.e., the existence of sin implies the existence of law. A popular assumption is that after Adam's life and until the events that occurred on Mt. Sinai, there was no written law or code that the people could follow. But since sin angered God and people were held accountable via the consequences that would occur if they didn't follow some kind of moral standard, survey says "something" was there from the time of Adam that helped the otherwise helpless humans recognize sin and avoid God's judgment. If not, then a lot of people incurred God's wrath and they couldn't have done a thing about it because they didn't know any better (which is unfair and not in line with God's character). And, since the Israelites couldn't send out a text blast or viral video at that time, the most reliable way to spread the word on rules they had to live by was to make sure that their fundamental laws were written down.

It can't be proven, but it's a believable theory that there was some kind of law in place before the Mosaic Law. Could that document have been the Noahide Law with its "justifiable homicide" clause called the *din rodef*?

Regardless of what ancient law, deliverance expectations, or internal conscience impulse that Moses may have been acting upon when he killed the Egyptian, we've looked at enough facts to come up with a responsible answer to our question of whether it was a justifiable act of defense or murder. The verdict?

It was *both*...

(Geez—this guy is even a misfit in court! He just doesn't belong *anywhere*!)

To the Egyptian courts, Moses would be seen as a traitorous killer. To the Jews, Moses would have been justified, if they only had known what, exactly, had taken place. He might have even been viewed as a hero to Israel if they could have only understood his motive, which they didn't (Acts 7:25). And this part is tragic: There is at least one Hebrew witness who accused Moses of murder, and for all we know, the majority of Israel would have been fed an inaccurate version of the story that paints Moses as a cold-blooded, calculated killer.

To his people, he had failed.

The rumors and gossip on both sides likely built an insurmountably grave reputation about Mr. Murder, Mr. Thou Shalt Not Kill, the defunct deliverer who says one thing with his mouth and does another with his blood-covered hands—the disappointment who might have been, and then wasn't, the man who would lead Israel to freedom.

Moses, Israel's hope and Egypt's pride, here donned the most ostentatious and brazen "misfit robe" to date in his life: Mr. Coward Fugitive...

Courageously, He... Ran Away?

He would be this to both of "his people"—you know, the two nations he was a grand leader over yesterday, but in which he would also never belong. Yeah. Those nations. He just failed both of their grand expectations and took on the label of "outlaw":

> Now when Pharaoh heard [of the Egyptian taskmaster's death], he sought to slay Moses. But Moses fled from the face of Pharaoh, and dwelt in the land of Midian. (Exodus 2:15)

In fact, he fled immediately, "at the saying" of the Hebrew who told him the event was witnessed (Exodus 2:14; Acts 7:29). He didn't gather his belongings, hug his favorite palace servants, brush his hair, roll up a sleeping bag, or kennel the cat for travel. Right then, right there, he fled as a criminal.

Part 2: The Floating Misfit

From that point on, or for at least the next forty years of his life (exactly double his current age), he would remain far away, second-guessing what he might have done differently, what he might have been. Because, if he, as Acts 2:75 states, already believed in his heart that there was a mutual deliverance understanding between himself and Israel, then the sudden redirect in his life no doubt would have been devastating, both for Moses and for the Hebrews. One day he was preparing to inherit the throne and commit the land to a social reformation (as far as they may have believed or expected), and the next he was a wanted man running from the law, incapable of ever rising to power in Egypt again.

But hold on. Just because others obviously would have perceived him as a coward because he fled "from the face of pharaoh," is that really who Moses was? Might there be another layer of beefy character to him that didn't involve pulling a weaselish move and abandoning everyone at this point in his life?

To be fair, there is that bit in the book of Hebrews that comes into play here as well. Note that the reflection into Hebrew and Greek that we've maintained up to this point has assisted us in the brackets below:

By faith Moses, when he was come to years [a fully grown man; the Greek here is "when he became great," or fully matured in judgment], refused [rather, self-denied] to be called the son of Pharaoh's daughter [much like a legal emancipation; he did not carry this out formally—he didn't "sign any papers"—but he never came back to the palace as a son of Bithiah]; Choosing rather to suffer affliction with the people of God, than to enjoy the pleasures of sin for a season [that is, the palace lifestyle would have been a sin had he continued to stay, now that he felt convicted to leave; this is not to suggest that his life in the palace during his youth was a sinful arrangement]; Esteeming the reproach of Christ [that is, the forthcoming Messiah, at the time of Moses] greater riches than the treasures in Egypt: for he had respect unto the recompence of the reward. By faith he forsook Egypt, not fearing the wrath of the king: for he endured, as seeing him who is invisible. (Hebrews 11:24–27)

So…which was it? Was Moses a coward, fleeing on a murder charge, leaving his poor bloodline to wallow in slavery and doing nothing about it to save his own hide? Or was he, like the writer of Hebrews states, "not fearing the wrath of the king," suddenly and boldly choosing to cast off the pleasures of the palace, become a pious ascetic, and throw himself into the afflictions of his people like a martyr…all while he just so happened to coincidently, conveniently, need to find a place and lay low for a while?

Well, that isn't exactly what Hebrews says. And no, there's more to it than that. This does puzzle some, though, so let's look at the timing.

Briefly, consider the context. Hebrews chapter 11 is called the "Hall of Faith" or "Faith Hall of Fame" for a reason. The writer reflects on quite a few heroes of the Old Testament in a long list, blasting the audience with one triumphant demonstration of faith after another by those whose reliance upon God assisted in building our very religion. The writer starts with Abel (the first martyr) and goes through the biggies— Enoch, Noah, Abraham, Sarah, Isaac, Jacob, Joseph, our man Moses, Joshua, Rahab, Gideon, Barak, Samson, Jephthah, David, and Samuel—before addressing several others through their stories, though not by name. All of these are in *one* chapter of the Word. Each transition from one character to another, and therefore from one epoch of time to another, are marked by the words, "By faith." So, as we're reading through the list, each time we see that phrase, we know we've jumped considerably in the timeline.

So yes, Moses did fear the face of Pharaoh, but in the healthy context of what Scripture describes, he feared the king because Moses' own death would have cut off the deliverer from his people! By the time we get to verse 27 in the Hall of Faith, we are no longer talking about a *forty-*

year-old Moses who just left (as we were the last three verses, 24–26); we are seeing a new era when Moses, age *eighty* now, has now forsaken all of Egypt and what it stands for in light of an invisible God whose wrath is far more fearsome than that of the Pharaoh. Put more simply: 1) Moses feared Pharaoh in the events described in Hebrews 11:24–26; 2) then we took a time leap, marked by the words "By faith"; 3) then Moses no longer feared Pharaoh during the events described in Hebrews 11:27 (forty years later), which we have yet to talk about. (A quick aside: For the skeptics online who got excited when they thought they found "a contradiction in the Bible," we want to encourage you: If at first you don't succeed, try and try again. The longer you look and the harder you try means the more convicting *Word of God* you've put into your mind, and that can't ever be a bad thing. Just one pointer, though: You may want to research your claim at least a little before you make videos about it, if you want to be taken seriously.)

As for why Moses is depicted in Hebrews as choosing to leave Egypt as a matter of conviction and Exodus 2:15 depicting it as a "flee" situation, the answer isn't as hard to determine as we may initially think. Scholars have long since figured this out, and the short answer is linked to a key event recorded in Exodus 2:11.

Remember earlier, when we talked about how Moses, though obviously aware of the slavery and the torment of his people, had no idea *how* bad it was until he visited them, "looked on their burdens," and then saw that beating? Scripture doesn't allow for any time between "looking on burdens" (realizing the extent of their torment) and taking in that shocking, "Egyptian-smiting-a-Hebrew" event. Moses was blasted with a lot of demoralizing information, then he outright killed a guy—a series of events that could mess with anybody. But, as we're told by Exodus 2:11's parallel verse over in Acts 7:23, none of this was Moses' idea: "And when he was full forty years old, *it came into his heart* to visit his brethren the children of Israel" (emphasis added). Moses wasn't out for a casual stroll. The event was preordained. All of our research turned up the unanimous belief that the means by which "it came into his heart" to check on his people was the Spirit of God; it wasn't an ordinary human impulse driven by emotion or curiosity. It was Moses' divine calling as a deliverer of the people that he would be led to them on this day, be instantly overwrought with angst at the realization of their burden, then have this imprint stamped in his mind by the sight of a brother killed under the scourge.

God showed him this. *Jehovah Almighty* inspired Moses to go out and see the state that his slave brethren were in. (Note that we're not saying God led Moses to kill.)

From there, the Word says, Moses had an entire night to think about it. He had all night to process and consider the evils he had seen enacted upon his poor people. Every moment, from the time he hid that body in the sand to the time he knew his crime had been witnessed, was one in which he had to think about who he was: who he was to God, to the Egyptians, to the Israelites, to his mother and father Jochebed and Amram, to Bithiah, to the royals in the court of Pharaoh…to everyone he had ever known, each of whom, Moses knew, had their own expectations. As the sun went down on one day and rose on another, Moses, who was led by the Spirit of God to see the oppression, was still being convicted by that same Lord. There is no doubt in the minds of these authors (and of many within the current and past world of academia) that the emotional and spiritual posture of Moses as described in Hebrews 11:24–26 had been taken on during this brief interlude. (Realistically speaking, that's the only place in the timeline this realization can take place. He wouldn't have chosen to leave before the event in Exodus 2:11, because he didn't yet know what he would need to be deeply aware of in order to take on the maturity of his feelings as described in Hebrews 11:24–26. But he couldn't have chosen to leave *after* the murder was discovered, as he left immediately and was on the run.)

So, beautifully, albeit indirectly, we're here given a sneak peek into the evening of that tragic day…

Part 2: The Floating Misfit

He had never known before how bad it was out there for his brothers and sisters, and now he had his wake-up call. He was ready now—even before he went to see the Hebrews again, he had begun to feel the winds of change rising within him, his spirit and heart alerting his senses that it was time to stop waiting and do something about Israel. While he was a child, he talked like a child and perceived like a child, but now as a man of forty, a man of fully matured judgment, he was obligated for the sake of God and man to put away childish things and concede to the duty bound through the deeper knowledge of these dual cultures he had been divinely exposed to for a lifetime. No longer could he stay in the palace while they were whipped and beaten outside. No longer could he accept being referred to as "the *prince* of Egypt," unless that title produced lasting relief for God's elect. The time had come, as he now felt in his spirit, that if it meant he would have to suffer, submitting himself to the afflictions of his people, he would rather do that than to be enticed to stay for a promise of palace-life convenience.

Such would be sin. And the weight of that realization had now fallen.

So, that grave night of the day that Moses had witnessed a murder and that he himself ended a life, he chose to either leave Egypt or use his office for the purpose of deliverance. The thoughts of challenging the head of Egypt or emancipating himself from its grip had taken deep root, and now it would be a matter of carrying out what he was convicted to do.

The next day, before he had a chance to make any other move, it was brought to his attention that someone had seen him kill another man, and Pharaoh would be out for blood. Moses feared for his life. It was a holy fear, a profound desperation to ensure that his actions wouldn't cut short the deliverer of all Israel...

...and then—and *only* then, after he had already decided to move ahead upon his fresh convictions—did he flee from the face of Pharaoh.[41]

Why did he leave so instantaneously? He was ready for such a departure...and in such a way that being "ready" would never depend on a suitcase.

But despite the strong motives behind his choice, his exit definitely created a buzz in both the Egyptian and the Israelite camps. It may not be expressly described in Scripture, but how could that *not* be what happened?

Here we have an entire nation of slaves watching one of their own grow up in the palace of the man who had the authority to free them, waiting and wondering if this Mr. Drawn from the Water guy just might be the means by which their deliverance from hell on earth would come, and then he killed someone and ran away. Not only that, but word on the street—at least from one Hebrew whose comment led to Moses' retreat—is that the killing had been a murder! Moses wasn't going to stick around and explain himself while the Pharaoh was in hot pursuit, so we can assume that even if there were groups of Hebrews who refused to believe their anointed deliverer was capable of homicide, there were others who were probably tearing their clothes and cursing the day Moses was born. The massive disappointment some must have felt is beyond anything we can think of in our modern, Western world.

And, according to the Egyptians, there was no doubt what their laws would decide regarding what Moses had done. They neither had, nor would've cared about, the rules/laws of justification that the Jews followed. No doubt, the story they were telling was that their prince had murdered a fellow Egyptian in cold blood and had fled the country.

Whether it was true or not—and biblically the case has been made that it was *not* true—Moses was now Mr. Coward.

The deliverer of the enslaved nation was a killer and a coward.

The Ten Commandment Man—the very one who would go on to deliver "Thou shalt not kill" as both a law and a means of proving one's integrity to God—was wanted for murder.

(Have we mentioned yet that Moses was a misfit?)

Part 2: The Floating Misfit

And That Was Only the Beginning...

Much of our character study thus far has involved a deep dive into Scripture and at least some speculation as to who the real Moses was, now that we've stripped away the Xerox-copy theology our culture has presented. Although we certainly could continue to unveil Moses at that level through the next several phases of his life, we'll refrain for one important reason: Those next periods are not central to his misfit image and qualities, and, therefore, aren't relevant to our purposes with this book. Let's watch the next part on fast-forward: Moses fled to the land of Midian, married, had a son, and became the shepherd of his father-in-law's flock (Exodus 2:15–25). (Oh yeah, also, the Pharaoh died, but the new guy who replaced him didn't care anymore than the last [2:23], so it hardly seems worth addressing further, except to point out that the Pharaoh Moses would someday challenge face to face would be someone other than his adopted grandfather-king.)

Whew.

Okay, let's slow back down for our climactic ending...

We join Moses again in Exodus 3:1, another forty years later (Acts 7:30), when he is eighty years old. (Times were different then, and human bodies withstood much less havoc wreaked upon them from such elements as pollution, radiation, abysmal "food" ingredients, and sedentary lifestyles; the truth is that, despite the warm feelings that we get when we hear sermons about God using "an old, *ooooold* man" to do the things Moses did, Moses wasn't that old for that time in history, and he was operating under the power and authority of God. There is no need to imagine that he was frail or feeble. Eighty then was today's fifty, you might say.)

After taking his flock far into the wilderness and to the foot of Mt. Sinai, Moses sees something extraordinary: a bush, consumed with fire, yet not burning up. Exodus 3:2 states that this was an appearance of "the Angel of the Lord," but this should be understood as the presence of God, Himself. Though scholars almost unanimously agree this is a theophany (when God appears as an angel), *Jamieson-Fausset-Brown* summarizes better than most that "it is clear that under this symbol, the Divine Being was present, whose name is given (Ex 3:4, 6), and elsewhere called the angel of the covenant."[42]

Right away, we have to pull the cartoon-bush concept out of the picture and replace it with something more realistic so we can appreciate the astonishing sight before Moses. This was *not* some plant with great amounts of greenery and moisture that could "hang in there" throughout the speech and then extinguish itself internally. (Seriously, some of the theories people come up with to "explain away" Scripture's supernaturalism is harder to believe than the miracle, you know? Geez...) The bushes, or *seneh* (Hebrew), scattered throughout that area were a specific, thorny species of acacia shrub; it was extremely dry and vulnerable to fire. In fact, it's known that it doesn't even need exposure to a flame to be ignited; even a nearby spark can set it ablaze. It has been reported that an acacia thorn bush fire can spread far and wide throughout a region as well.[43] So, seeing this type of plant on fire, then watching it long enough to make the statement that the bush was on fire but not consumed, would have indeed been quite a sight, as Scripture acknowledges.

Moses stops what he is doing and wanders over to the bush, just as the voice of God rings out from it, calling his name and instructing him to remove his sandals as he approaches the holy ground. (By the way: The Eastern origins of the footwear removal—as it is specific to worship [not as it relates to royalty, as there were similar customs in that regard, although for unrelated reasons]—identify the worshiper as a servant to his god, as well as a make "confession of personal defilement and conscious unworthiness to stand in the presence of unspotted holiness."[44]) God identifies Himself as "the God of thy father, the God of Abraham, the God of Isaac, and the God of Jacob" (Exodus 3:6), establishing that the voice Moses is hearing is not a hallucination or some other entity. Meanwhile, Moses, afraid to look upon God, hides his face. We will, as we did before, take the following words verse by verse and with clarifying comments included in brackets:

> And the Lord said, "I have surely seen the affliction of my people which are in Egypt, and have heard their cry by reason of their taskmasters [note that, interestingly, even God, Himself, acknowledges the central reason for the "cry" of the Israelites is the beatings given by the slave drivers; it is surprising that the one Hebrew accused Moses of murder for his act of vengeance, but perhaps this is why Moses didn't think the people understood his motive (Acts 7:25)]; for I know their sorrows; And I am come down to deliver them out of the hand of the Egyptians [crucially important: God, Himself—not Moses–has come down to deliver them; we will come back to this in a moment], and to bring them up out of that land unto a good land and a large, unto a land flowing with milk [typical in this area and historical period, the milk would have been goat's, suggesting the land was suitable for many goats to feed, unlike the wilderness deserts around Sinai] and honey [likely referring to the honey that would have been made from dates, which suggests the land of Canaan would have been ripe with date trees]; unto the place of the Canaanites, and the Hittites, and the Amorites, and the Perizzites, and the Hivites, and the Jebusites. Now therefore, behold, the cry of the children of Israel is come unto me: and I have also seen the oppression wherewith the Egyptians oppress them. Come now therefore, and I will send thee unto Pharaoh, that thou mayest bring forth my people the children of Israel out of Egypt. (Exodus 3:7–10)

Don't miss this beautiful, astounding moment in the Word. Here's God, admitting with His own voice that He, Himself, will be the Deliverer (verse 8). Initially, this sounds like a great plan to our stuttering friend who may have believed in this moment that he was personally off the hook. We addressed at length already the likelihood that Moses knew he was both Hebrew *and* deliverer, since he "supposed his brethren [at the time of the murder accusation] would have understood how that God by his hand would deliver them" (Acts 7:25). Now God is saying *He's* going to take care of it. Wow, no offense to Moses (and he would certainly agree), but this seems like a much better plan! It's not that Moses is an incompetent man—goodness knows, forty years of studies at the palace to be trained in all the wisdom of the Egyptians (Acts 7:22–23) is excellent preparation for anyone who would challenge the Pharaoh to let God's people go. No argument here. But God? That's such a great idea! Who needs Moses when there's God to—

Oh, hang on a sec. See verse 10?

> Come now therefore, and *I will send thee* [Moses] unto Pharaoh, that thou mayest bring forth my people the children of Israel out of Egypt.

Yup. That would be God, by His own admission, stating that Moses will be the human conduit *through* whom God operates in divine wisdom, power, and authority, ultimately obliterating the shackles of Israel and leading them out of Egypt.

Do you get it? When *God* says something is going to happen through one of His misfits, it doesn't happen because the misfit is qualified. It happens because God is the Almighty Crusher of anything He wants crushed, and nobody can stand against Him! Defeating the greatest powers in the history of all regions of hell requires less effort for our Powerful Creator than toppling a tower of onion rings.

Moses didn't get it:

> And Moses said unto God, "Who am I, that I should go unto Pharaoh, and that I should bring forth the children of Israel out of Egypt?" (Exodus 3: 11)

He's believed his entire life (or at least that's what the majority of evidence suggests) that he will be the deliverer, and now, he's balking. Why? Doesn't he believe that God is capable of doing all that He said? Isn't it obvious—by the flaming acacia thorn bush in front of his face, if not by any other sign—that God is more dependably commanding over all forces upon the earth than any other being, and can therefore be trusted to follow through on His claims? Does Moses doubt for some reason that God's nature is immutable and, as such, that He would be incapable of promising something with no intent to follow through?

What inside Moses is quirkily ticking to make him say such a thing to the very presence of God as, "Who am *I* to do this deliverance thing?" Why does Moses doubt what God has planned or question how God intends to use humans to carry out His plan?

But of course, if you're familiar with the story, you know it's not the last time this kind of arguing-with-God tactic is tried and fails. It's kind of Moses' *modus operandi*. This is true even though God tells Moses that He will be with him the entire time (v. 12). God goes as far as to tell Moses exactly what to say to the Israelites and the Pharaoh (vv. 13–18).

When a man with a stutter is given the rare opportunity to have words put right in his mouth by God Almighty, whose transcendent presence guarantees that the message is delivered seamlessly and with all the power needed to influence the recipient, you would *think* he'd be all over that offer. But alas, no. The misfit is so unwilling to believe in his human qualifications that he argues again:

And Moses answered and said, "But, behold, they will not believe me, nor hearken unto my voice: for they will say, The Lord hath not appeared unto thee." (Exodus 4:1)

God—whose Voice is still coming from a burning bush that isn't burning, by the way—tells Moses to throw down his staff. By the power of our Lord, the staff becomes a snake, a miraculous display for Moses, right there on the spot, to prove that He Who Calls is qualified enough for both of them to carry out the promised calling. Moses jumps away from the snake, but the Voice coming from the bush directs him to lift it by the tail, and, upon doing so, he is left once again with staff in hand. Another miracle. God, taking it a step further, informs Moses that *he* will be able to perform this snake wonder in the sight of any and all Israelites to establish that he has truly been sent by God.

We beg you: Don't do as many Christians and skim over the implications of this. This is the moment God illustrates, as a fact, that a miracle can be done "by Him, but *through* man." Back in Exodus 3:7, God told Moses that *He* had come down to do all the delivering…and in verse 10, Moses learns that it will be done through *him* as God's servant. Then Moses doubts and argues, as is his nature around this time in his life, and God in a sense "loans him" a miracle that he can now perform by God's power. It's hard to understand why Moses is still insisting that he isn't worthy.

Come on, readers. Accept the conviction. Know that we're making a point to *you* through all of this. Some of you, even right now, are reading this and thinking: *This works for other, more important people, but who am I? God can't possibly expect* me, *of all people, to perform these things He's told me to do.*

See, that's the beauty of it all. He's not expecting "you" to. He's going to do it. *He* is. Not you. He's just asking you to be useable in the execution of what *He* is doing. Don't be a Moses. Don't waste that kind of time while there is a calling on your life and lost souls waiting for you to answer it.

Need more convincing? Mkay…

God then performs a third miracle, instructing Moses to reach inside his cloak. Moses obeys, and when he pulls his hand out again, it's white as snow from leprosy. And yes, we said "third miracle." People frequently and erroneously refer to this event as the "second" miracle, but if we're going to be technical, it's the second *sign*. If God's power hadn't turned the snake back into a staff, the story of Moses might have gotten to this point and ended with a venom-induced poisoning. This is the *third* time God has proven Himself to Moses, though He should never have had to. Miracle number four comes immediately in the form of a healing when Moses, by the Lord's instruction, reaches in and out of his cloak again and his hand is restored to health. In modern language, what God says to Moses next is, "If they don't believe you by the first sign, they will by the time you've shown them the second" (Exodus 4:8). However—and this is mind-boggling—God goes on to say in verse 9 that if they still don't believe, Moses has the authority by the power of God to take some water from the Nile and pour it on the ground, whereupon it will turn to blood.

Even with all of this in his arsenal, Mr. Misfit continues to argue with God:

And Moses said unto the Lord, "O my Lord, I am not eloquent, neither heretofore, nor since thou hast spoken unto thy servant: but I am slow of speech, and of a slow tongue." (Exodus 4:11)

You have to admit this is rather unbelievable. Moses has seen more supernatural activity in five minutes than most of us would ever see in seven lifetimes, but he still can't get over his own feelings of inadequacy. He has believed since at least the time of the murder accusation that it would be through his own hand that God would deliver His people. But when the rubber meets the road at Sinai, Moses uses everything he's got, including his stutter, to show the Lord he's not worthy.

At this point in the narrative we can almost hear the irritation building in God's voice:

And the Lord said unto him, "who hath made man's mouth? or who maketh the dumb, or deaf, or the seeing, or the blind? have not I the Lord? Now therefore go, and I will be with thy mouth, and teach thee what thou shalt say." (Exodus 4:11–12)

Imagine the tone here. "Who *made* your tongue, Moses!? Who gave you your stutter in the first place!? It was *Me*! Don't question Me! Don't lecture Me about your weaknesses, as *I'm powerful enough* to keep any of them from stopping me in this! Now go do what I've told you to do! I will make sure you articulate smoothly, and don't worry about what to say, either. I'll give you every word."

Moses, Moses, Moses. For a guy who can hardly speak, he sure protests up a storm on *this* day. Believe it or not, in one final plea, Moses begs God: "O my Lord, send, I pray thee, by the hand of him whom thou wilt send" (Exodus 4:13). Scholars are unanimous in stating that this, in modern words, would read, "Lord, please! Just send *anyone* else!" Moses has abandoned giving any reasoning for his inadequacies and has resorted to simply pleading that God will find someone else, someone more qualified.

Tragically, Moses' critical self-doubt wins. God agrees to send his Hebrew brother, Aaron, to go along with him to speak. This is carried out as the official plan...

...robbing Moses forever of the *fullness* of the honor God initially wanted to bestow upon him.

You probably know the rest of the story. Moses and Aaron repeatedly challenge Pharaoh to let the Hebrews go free, and as the ruler refuses, ten horrible, frightening demonstrations of God's power are released upon Egypt. The Nile is turned to blood, followed by plagues of frogs, gnats, and flies, trailed by the death of all Egyptian livestock. Then, blistering boils erupt on the skin of Egyptian animals and people, the worst hailstorm in Egypt's history destroys the land and kills anyone who is outside, and locusts swarm in giant clouds and eat anything left in the fields that the hail hasn't devastated. Darkness falls across the nation for three straight days...then the angel of death claims the life of every firstborn son. (Not one Israelite is affected by any of this. God's people, who are living in a small town called Goshen, are protected entirely from the catastrophe.)

Part 2: The Floating Misfit

All the while, despite his stutter, despite his murder charges, despite the fact that he ran away and earned the "coward" label amidst both cultures, Moses is at the center of every promise, every threat, and every action taken by God in wrath against the Egyptians.

The night the angel of death takes the life of Pharaoh's son, the king finally relents and allows the Israelites to leave. But when the full consequence of that decision dawns on him shortly thereafter, he takes every chariot left in the kingdom and pursues the Israelites with maximum military power, cornering them at the Red Sea. God tells Moses to raise his staff over the sea and part the waters, and when he obeys, the Israelites walk between the giant walls of water on dry ground.

Once again, Mr. Coward is at front and center of the movement of God, bravely carrying out the order of his Commander.

On the other side of the sea, Moses, following the prompting of God, raises his staff again, and the waters crash back down upon the Egyptians in pursuit. Not one of their number survives, not even Pharaoh.

Once again, Mr. No Name leads his people by the power of the God who has always known exactly who he is and what he's called for.

When the people arrive at Sinai, God gives Moses the Law, including the Ten Commandments that will convict every hearer from this day forward, reform all of humanity forever, and establish the Sovereign Lord as the true Wise Ruler of all lands, peoples, and cultures for all time.

And once again, Mr. Stutter is the mouthpiece through whom God speaks.

Countless miracles have occurred since. Entire nations have risen and fallen from Moses' day until now. Incalculable world-changing events have taken place, and a limitless number of people have been born into a calling, carried it out well, and gone to be with the Lord.

But the world will never forget the man:

- Who would never be known by his covenant name;
- Who wasn't sensationally carried over the rushing rapids in a wicker basket;
- Who wasn't an Egyptian, but wasn't a Hebrew;
- Who couldn't speak without difficulty but whom God asked to be a prolific public orator;
- Who was asked to tell others to never commit murder, though he was wanted for that very crime because he killed someone he may not have murdered;
- Who fled but who wasn't a coward;
- Who couldn't be used by God to liberate the Israelites but who fulfilled his calling as the deliverer of Israel;
- Whose biography repeatedly proved to not be worth telling, but whose story has been used by God in bewilderingly miraculous ways an infinite number of times and will never stop being one of the most popular and inspiring account in human history.

Mr. Misfit.

Part 3

Stepping Off the Island

The key to beginning to grow spiritually—as an individual, as a Church, and in ministry—is by realizing and embracing the fact that we're not all cut from the same cloth. In fact, our greatest strengths are often found in our diversities and eccentricities. God did not invite us into His Kingdom to homogenize us into a congregation of cookie-cutter followers. He created a population of unique people who, when united under His purposes, can serve Him with a fuller and more thorough capacity than we ever can when we live under the scrutiny of trying to be like others. Once we embrace our inner oddball, we become free to find His identity for us and His calling on our lives, and we can even discover the fullness of our own unique way of serving Him. By allowing ourselves to find the misfit within, we become free to experience the distinctive abundance that He has for each of us; we begin to live our *own* story.

4

Meet the Toys & Friends

By Allie Henson

To present a book that refers constantly to the characters from the Island of Misfit Toys in *Rudolph the Red-Nosed Reindeer* but never individually studies them would be similar to hanging an ornate but empty frame on a wall. The color, undertones, and even overarching picture would be missed. Yet, the intricacies that set apart these toys are often so minute that those who watched the film as a child may remember the misfits, but not what made them outcasts.

Therein lies the crux of much of our work in this book: Although each plaything has individual peculiarities, the truth is, none of them had anything so wrong that they deserved the dark fate of being banished from the rest of the world. And, while many of us can relate to these oddballs, we're often quicker to see their redeemability than we are to recognize our own loveable qualities. Yet, we're not so different from these icons of Christmas.

In other words, each of us can see reflections of our own shortcomings in the unconventionalities of these toys. But, while we're usually quick to overlook flaws in others—toys included—we typically, based on the very same perceived defects, isolate ourselves from others. We permit other people to be imperfect, but grant ourselves no such luxury.

By looking at each of the toys, we hope to bring this self-segregating discrepancy to light and help the reverse this destructive habit. After all, many of the quirks, when viewed from the proper angle, can be recognized as strengths rather than weaknesses.

A ~~Jack~~ Charlie-in-the-Box?

In the world of misfit toys, it quickly becomes apparent that simply deviating from tradition is enough to render one as an outcast. For example, a toy that has always been called "Jack"-in-the-Box becomes ostracized when, instead, the character inside is called "Charlie." Certainly, for the onlooker, this is no big problem: One can play with a "Charlie"-in-the-Box just as easily as one can with a "Jack"-in-the-Box. So what's the real problem here?

The question is answered by Charlie himself: "*Who* wants a Charlie-in-the-Box?"[45] The irony of this is that it doesn't seem to cross anyone else's mind to be upset that his name is Charlie. The title-shaming here is completely self-imposed. It's likely that if Charlie simply jumped out of the box and greeted onlookers with a mere "Hello, I'm a Charlie-in-the-box!" nobody would really mind at all.

So how does this connect to readers? It's simple: We self-label every day, branding ourselves with names accrued usually through negative experiences. We say we're "abandoned," "addicted," "rejected," "bullied," "insufficient," "unattractive," "unintelligent," or just plain "damaged." Then we stand in proximity to others and ask ourselves, just as Charlie did, "Who wants a [insert self-imposed, self-abasing name here]?" We continually put ourselves through this, even though if we would just present ourselves with confidence, most people wouldn't notice our shortcomings—and those who do would likely find them relatable.

What is *your* self-imposed name, the one you allow to hold you down? What is the label by which you've chosen to limit your own potential? Is it something that derives from victimization of the past? Does it spring from a hurtful label that an abusive parent, spouse, employer, or other person has placed on you? Perhaps it's the label of a past failure or a situation you wish you had handled differently: "school dropout," "divorcee," "deadbeat," or "quitter." Maybe it's a physical attribute you're self-conscious about. Ultimately, what we perceive as shortcomings doesn't matter. In fact, the less equipped we, with our human limitations, feel we are for a job, the more God is glorified in our success.

Our past failures are no longer important. The label we've painted on our chest doesn't matter. What *does* matter is whether God has called, chosen, and thus prepared us for a certain task.

Deciding to step out in faith and allow God to redefine us can be the first hurdle we cross toward forever abandoning a negative marker or self-inflicted, painful name. Understand that the Maker of us all has the transformative power to make us a new creation (2 Corinthians 5:17). Believing this helps us realize that this promise not only applies to those around us, but is also true about ourselves.

And, here is the best part: God will change the name of the forsaken, the desolate, to a new name, which will be one of belonging (Isaiah 62:2–5). He has changed the names of many people in the past whose destinies were rewritten by His mighty hand. Abram and Sarai became Abraham and Sarah (Genesis 17); Jacob became Israel (Genesis 32); Simon became Peter (John 1); and even Paul took on a new name when he began his ministry (Acts 13). And, God's people will each have their names written in the Lamb's Book of Life to spend eternity with Him (Revelation 20:15).

So, what's in a name?

The same God who has chosen you and ordained you for His work has the power to change the name that defines you. And, if the Author of all of creation exercises His prerogative of making such an adaptation, then who are we to argue with that? Will we stand before him, insisting that this can't be done, stating that we are more damaged than even He realizes? Of course not.

Ironically, Charlie-in-the-Box is the first on the island to interact with Rudolph and Cornelius. He is presented as the official sentry of the island. Despite his erroneous title, he proves to be a capable fellow of esteem: the guardian, the sentinel, the watchman for all who reside on the isle. The only person seemingly hung up on his name is Charlie, himself. He is blinded by his inability to see past something as silly as a label, but it is apparent that those who rely on him see an able-bodied and proficient individual whom they trust. Perhaps he should have been renamed "Sentry." While the film didn't officially reintroduce him with this label, for all practical purposes, this is precisely what happened.

Often, because we can't see the honorable names placed upon us by others, such as Charlie's "Sentry," we confine ourselves within a box. While it may be true that the cubicle itself is a permanent part of the toy's function, it doesn't need to be the darkened place into which he continually retreats. Charlie is given a choice: He can open the top of his box and come springing out so that he can intermingle with those around him and live life to its fullest, or he can choose to retreat into the container, clamp the lid shut, and stay there all alone. Unfortunately, when we hide in this way, we live cut off from the outside. We neither improve the world around us nor gain from it. We find ourselves sequestered in a shadowy and desolate place. And, many of us live this way each day because we are unable to relinquish a damaging label. We lack the courage it takes to walk with confidence into a world of other like-wise damaged and hurting people and say, "Hello, my name is Charlie. Nice to meet you!"

Such an act of bravery may seem easier said than done, but many of the people who do this very thing each day do so because they have intentionally chosen to leave their comfort zone behind, shed the damaging label of their past, and participate in a more abundant life.

Seeing Spots: The Elephant with Dots

After a while, *Rudolph* viewers may begin to notice a pattern emerge among the misfit toys. Essentially, each one seems to be different from their peers in a way that—while not fully impeding its functionality—changes the way it is played with or makes it feel self-conscious. In this way, it seems obvious that the spotted elephant is an outcast because he perceives himself to be one; he feels as though he sticks out like a sore thumb in a world of solid-colored peers.

As with the other toys, this unconventionality may not bother a child at all. Thus, the only thing stopping this toy from doing the same things as the others is, like Charlie, his own inability to see beyond what he perceives as a flaw. But, unlike Charlie, who at least looks similar to his Jack-named counterparts, our four-legged friend bears a visible marker that causes him to withdraw. This sheds a different light on our "label." And, this can be debilitating regardless of whether or not our spots are noticeable to those around us.

Such an element can manifest in many different ways. For some, it might be a physical difference or even a handicap that people are self-conscious about. Others might feel certain that experiences of their past—whether they were an actor or a victim—are easily detected by others. In order to keep this imprint hidden, they recoil. While Charlie's hindrance is an internal label, the spotted elephant feeds off of something he believes to be perceptibly different about himself that keeps him isolated.

Often, the "differences" we notice right away when comparing ourselves to others are invisible to those around us. I will pick on myself a bit to illustrate this point. When I was a teenager, fashion-modeling schools were all the rage. I attended one, landed some modeling jobs after I graduated, and was actively involved with a modeling agency for a while. People often associate such a claim with fame or wealth, but I never made much money at it. (In fact, it's not uncommon for new models to be paid with "exposure" rather than wages. Essentially, those in this line of work know that fresh recruits are hungry for experience, so this becomes a form of exploitation.) Many people subscribe to the notion that anyone who is pretty can be a model. But this isn't necessarily true. First, there is the fact that the modeling and film industries usually prefer women who are, at most, somewhere between a size 0 and a 2, regardless of how attractive they are. Additionally, there is much more to modeling than looking pretty in front of a camera. To be successful, models must have a unique look; understand the strengths and weaknesses of their body and how to face the camera (thus they know how to pose); know how to walk a runway; be confident, professional, and appealing during interviews; and have access to the financial resources it takes to build a great portfolio. On top of this, models must have thick enough skin to endure being cruelly rejected from auditions (openly referred to as "cattle calls") over, and over, and over. (Some may say the industry has changed in the thirty years since I navigated it. I certainly hope that's true, but this is how it was for me.)

As a teenager, I was a size 6 and nearly 5'9" tall. This meant that while, by many standards, I was slender, to those within the fashion modeling industry, I was considered pretty chunky. I was, on many occasions, told I needed to lose weight; for a long time I tried earnestly to do so. I'll never forget one day when I and several other would-be models at an audition were told to line up against a wall—while facing it. We were to put our hands up on the wall near our heads, almost as though we were about to be frisked by a police officer. The man interviewing us came by and placed his hands on either side of each person's waist, quickly patting each of us above the hip bone. It wasn't a lingering contact—rather, it was a quick motion that was over in less than a second. As he made his way down the line, his words to each woman being rejected were, "Too fat." He made his way from one girl to the next: "Too fat...too fat...too fat..." A couple of young women, instead of hearing this repeated phrase, simply were told, "Okay."

Part 3: Stepping Off the Island

When the man had made his way past everybody in the room, he pointed only to those he had not said "too fat" to; everyone else was dismissed.

I share this because, during the teenage years, many young women base much of their value on their appearance. A woman can be raised in church, have great parents, be part of a loving social group, or have access to myriad other nurturing resources, but our culture will still make a lot of beautiful young women (and men, for that matter!) believe that their appearance features some monstrosity that devalues their worth. These are often characteristics that peers and family vehemently say aren't noticeable, but to them, they're glaringly dominating when they look into a mirror.

As a young woman who had been exposed to such criticism, my "spots" quickly became my weight. And, while friends and family told me that I shouldn't worry about my weight (which, at the time, hovered between 125 and 130 pounds) all I could see in my reflection was a distorted self-image covered in cellulite and fat rolls. Conversely, I could look at someone larger than me who might be complaining about her appearance, and I could see her loveliness that extended far beyond her body type. When I told other girls that they were beautiful just the way they were, I meant it—every time—from the bottom of my heart. It was as though I had two standards, two sets of eyes: those that saw everyone else through a lens of grace and those that saw myself through a lens of criticism and cruelty.

I later learned that, at that point of my life, much of the reason I had so much trouble losing weight was the simple fact that I had very little body fat in the first place. In fact, I was basically formed of muscle mass and bone. I grew self-conscious, but kept up an appearance of confidence. I felt disgusting and valueless, and I was always looking for ways to balance the façade of confidence against my need to shrink away from attention. I compared myself to others constantly. It even became hard for me to eat in front of others, because I felt as though I could hear their thoughts as they watched me:

"Gross. She's actually taking another bite. That's, seriously, like the fourth bite. How many does the glutton plan on taking? Ugh. I can't watch. This is disgusting."

I can't tell you how many times I sat at a meal with someone and I talked, smiled, laughed, and otherwise kept up the "I'm fine" act, but inwardly, my companion's words weren't even registering. All I could hear were the degrading words I've just mentioned. All of this tortured me almost constantly, while those around me had no way of knowing about my mental battle. I played the "comparison game" in my head the entire time I was in a room with any other women.

She's taller. She's skinnier. She has prettier hair. Her teeth are straighter than mine. Her teeth are whiter than mine. Her eyelashes are longer.

I mean really. The list went on and on. You see, it doesn't matter how many attractive attributes you have or how many flaws you have. Reader, please hear me on this, because I learned it the hard way: If you only see the beauty of other people and the flaws of yourself, you *never* win the comparison game.

My deteriorating self-image exacerbated as I entered my adult life, and by the time I reached my early twenties, fixing my post-baby body nearly became an obsession. In fact, at one point, I followed a trending diet so hard and for so long that I had a seizure as a result of a serious deficiency in key nutrients.

What finally helped me—ironically—wasn't that this health issue manifested as a result of dieting. It was the brutal lecture the doctor who diagnosed my seizure event gave me. I'm telling you, this guy pulled no punches. In fact, when I've retold the story in detail, people are often indignant at his lack of bedside manners and the tone he took with me. All I can say is that what he said was precisely what I needed to hear in order to change the trajectory of my life. He asked me if I was so selfish that I would be happy to let my loved ones (including my kids) bury me as long as I was cute when they put me in the ground. I had never thought of it that way. It never occurred to me that I was being "selfish," but that was the word the doctor used. I was stunned—part of me wanted to argue with him, but everything he said to me was fair, and I found myself respecting him for his willingness to speak truth. With this newfound point of view, it also began to occur to me that I had been isolating myself from the rest of the world; many people didn't know the real me. They knew an appearance of togetherness that I let them see, not the vulnerable, insecure girl hiding inside. I showed them a carefully crafted picture while drawing assumptions about them as well. (Later, there was a landmark day in my life when I began to say "I am secure enough to admit my insecurities." It may not sound like much to others, but it was huge progress for me.)

I returned to that doctor several times for follow-up care. On a different visit, another event is etched into my memory that, like his lecture, permanently changed the path of my life. I was sitting in the waiting room, reading a magazine article that was an exposé on women who had competed in beauty pageants. The article highlighted one of the main pageant winners by discussing physical augmentation that she'd had done, and it featured before-and-after pictures of her. I soon realized that the only part of her face that appeared to be originally intact was her bottom lip; her "before" picture looked much like any typical woman you might run into at the grocery store, standing there in sweats with her hair scrunched up in a ponytail. While I don't remember the names of the competitors or other details about their cosmetic surgeries, I will never forget the realization I had that day: Each of us playing the comparison game is buying into a grandiose lie.

Now, before continuing, I must acknowledge that both the modeling industry and Hollywood are filled with people who are beautiful. But, these people have an entirely different toolbox available than those of us on the outside world have. Many have cosmetic surgeons, cosmetologists, makeup artists, beauticians, fashion artists, tailors, personal trainers, and lots of other resources, along with time and money at their disposal that can all be poured into improving their appearance. And since, for many, their appearance directly correlates to their livelihood, their physical exterior becomes a very high priority. Conversely, neglecting the way they look can mean they'll be ostracized or have difficulty finding work. I'm certainly not faulting people in the modeling and acting fields for their need to place high importance on their looks. I'm just stating the cold, hard fact about the world they navigate. Thus, my point is not to pick on anyone. However, for years, I tried to look like them when I didn't have the resources and tools they had. I daresay most people *could* look like part of that world if such means were within their grasp.

I realize that I've been talking more about women than men (obviously, because I had this experience as a young woman), but people of both genders and all walks of life can feel a sense of failure attached to appearance that can literally hinder their desire to mingle in a room full of people. And while my story has to do with the fact that I'm not a size 0, this issue can manifest in nearly any trait (whether it's one's fitness, height, complexion, or anything ese) that makes a person physically uncomfortable or self-conscious in a room full of other people. For a man, it could be that he wishes for more muscle bulk. It could be an individual's height if they are particularly tall or short. It could have to do with acne or obesity. Or, the issue could be something that the person perceives as visible, but that others don't even notice.

For those of us who are only now recognizing how our own "spots" have kept us divided from others, the charge is simple: Learn a new way of defining your spots. For me, it was that "aha moment" when I realized that many celebrities look just like we all do before the professionals go to work on them. I never did become a size 0; in fact, I gave that goal up completely. I'm now a size 12, and have been for more than twenty years. This is as small as I get while maintaining my health, and my size is likely never going to change, unless it goes up. It's just how God created me.

I found contentment not by "fixing" what I perceived to be "wrong" about my body by removing my "spots." Instead, I learned to adjust my perspective about my true assets and decide what priority I should give my dissatisfaction with my "flaws." (This came when that doctor, as I shared earlier, asked if it was important enough to be skinny at the risk of letting my children grow up without a mother; all while I realized that the difference in many of us and those in Hollywood was a simple matter of resources.)

Ultimately, I was finally able to step out of the comparison game. I'll always be able to find characteristics of other people that I would like to have for myself, and there may be qualities in me that others might wish for as well. But, at the end of the day, none of these evaluations matter, nor do they bring fulfillment. Even if I could complete my checklist of things I would love to change about myself today, I would only make a new list tomorrow. We can take the whole gamut of measures that will make us feel beautiful or successful, and the very next day find a list of other imperfections we want to correct. Most of the time, such matters fall pretty low on the priority list when eternal appraisals are being made—and these are the comparisons we *should* be making. The rest is fleeting. At the end of our lives, all that matters is how well we live spiritually, how we serve, and who we share our message with.

I've shared much about my own story, so I will also tell you about the deliverance that the Lord brought into my life on this matter. Since this experience more than twenty years ago, I've learned to laugh at myself. I was recently in the green room of a large television network preparing to go on the air. I was brushing my hair when the woman who came to help with my makeup commented on the "pretty color of golden blonde" my hair is.

"Thanks, it's Garnier Fructis' 1000, chamomile," I blurted.

Did I mention I've learned to laugh at myself?

The woman who paid me the compliment appeared confused, while a bystander said, "It sounds like you spend more money on your shampoo than I do."

"Oh no," I responded. "That's not shampoo. That's my hair dye."

A brief moment of silence followed. As the recognition began to register on both women's faces, I leaned out to my side so that my hair would hang down loosely, away from my shoulders. I took my hand and opened it, palm side up, and placed it near my head. I slowly and dramatically ran my hand—still palm side up—down the length of my hair, gesturing much like a spokesmodel holding a cosmetic product in an old TV game show would do. Then I pointed very closely at the darker roots peaking up from my scalp.

I smiled sarcastically, and said, "See it? This ain't real…"

After a moment, the women recovered from my unexpected candor. We all enjoyed a good laugh, but nobody could have understood the kind of courage such bold openness would've taken me twenty years ago. The reason I was able to advertise (and even now, put into print!) the fact that my usually dishwater-blonde-speckled-with-some-gray hair has such a golden tone is because I regularly get some help from the local drugstore. But, it's this kind of transparency that will help people playing the comparison game to finally realize that everybody is using whatever tools they have available. When we spend our energy trying to size up whether we compare to those around us, we focus on the wrong priorities, limit ourselves unnecessarily, punish ourselves undeservedly, and ultimately waste energy that could be spent on pursuits that have eternal meaning. We simply must place our flaws in their proper perspective, because it's likely that we ourselves are the only ones hung up on these "shortcomings" in the first place.

What's Wrong with Her? Sue's Dolly

The dolly for Sue. A cute little rag doll who sings, smiles, and plays well with others on the island. The million-dollar question on everyone's mind when watching this show is, "Just what is wrong with *that* toy, anyway?"

Part 3: Stepping Off the Island

Despite Rudolph-creator Rankin apparently joking at one point that this doll had been abandoned, the truth is, this question has gone largely unanswered. All we know is that, one day, she or someone else decided that she was less than desirable, and so was banished to the isle. Another toy amongst the group of exiles—a bird who swims instead of flying—is seen floating in the background of scenes, literally. Could these two oddballs have something in common?

I would wager that they do. Some people—both those who stand out as fish-out-of-water types and those who look like they fit in just fine—can be plagued by the nagging suspicion that they simply don't fit in. The reason could be as simple as perhaps their knowledge that they are operating outside of their optimal avenue of calling, or it could be that their interests, personality style, or even demographics don't quite match their own background.

I'll never forget watching my mom operate as a pastor's wife and helpmate to my dad. For years, I watched her efforts at balance while her perceived role of duty and her truer identity—you know, the one that intertwines with your calling—didn't completely align with one another. To be clear, it wasn't that her role as my dad's helper and partner necessarily opposed who she was truly meant to be, it's just that while it was playing out, she was unable to see how the one contributed to the other, and vice versa. Only after years of dedicated obedience to God's calling did she realize how her faithfulness in one avenue (duty) would open the door for the calling that connected to her truer identity. And during that time, despite her efforts, she somehow could never escape the awkward feeling that she just didn't quite fit in. Allow me to explain.

For those who have read my mom's book, *No Fences: It Started with a Plastic Pony*, it is quickly apparent that she is a farm girl, through and through. When she wasn't playing with toy horses as a little girl, she was imagining them, drawing them, or—if she was lucky—interacting with the real thing. She gave her life to God during her young adulthood, and soon after married my dad. The two decided to enter the ministry. While this vocation should be affected only by the noble cause of the Great Commission, it is at times, unfortunately, filled with other dynamics as well. In fact, within the field of ministry, there are some who make it all about politics; others in ministry see themselves as heroes; and still others use the ministry as a veil behind which they seek—through their own means—to redeem past mistakes but forget to bring God along in their endeavors. In short, while there are many devout and well-meaning people in this line of work, there are also flawed and misled human beings whose expectations for themselves and each other can bring about mishaps.

I grew up watching both my parents navigate this arena with as much grace as people can muster. Those in ministry live under the great constraints that people themselves attach to such roles, which can impede a person's true ability to connect with oneself. For my mom, there were parts of her life that simply took a back burner during those years. For example, the farm-girl hat went on a back hat rack while she donned the official uniform of nearly every pastor's wife in the 1980s: a below-the-knee, straight-cut skirt with matching blazer. The long, country-girl hair was cut, layered and rolled into perm rods, rendering the pre-approved, cookie cutter, "minister's wife hairdo" sported by nearly every woman in this position during that decade. She wore it well, but those who *really* knew her were aware the fit was a little "off."

As another example, my mom can take a set of drums for a serious run. Several years ago, my parents renewed their wedding vows for their fortieth anniversary. All the BFG (Broken for Good with Joe Horn) band members brought their instruments and jammed out during the reception. There was Nita Horn, decked to the nines in her lacy wedding gown, a giant cloud of billowing, white pouf spread out behind a set of drums; her jaw was squared as her determined eyes focused on her hands moving the drumsticks faster than most people can even visually follow. Seeing such a sight was a first for everyone in attendance: the bride drumming the song "Wipeout;" tearing it up without mercy, while a crowd of onlookers saw a side of Nita Horn that they didn't know existed.

Yet, when I was very young, Mom stopped drumming for a season. Some of the early churches my dad worked in were hyperconservative; they deemed it unladylike for a woman to wear pants. However, it was equally indelicate to sit and work the leg pedals on a set of drums while wearing a dress. Then, there were those who thought it inappropriate for a woman to play drums at all. Others didn't mind a female playing drums, but considered it an undignified activity for a pastor's wife. And, this was in churches that would allow drums in the first place, as opposed to those that perceived the whole notion of adding rhythm to the music to be a little too close to rock-and-roll for comfort in their own assembly.

Thus, Mom repeatedly relinquished the opportunity to play drums, and for years didn't even own a set.

Another way Mom worked to fill the role of a godly woman in leadership was in the way she presented herself. In some churches, it was believed that cosmetics were the work of a Jezebel, so she abstained from applying a drop of makeup. In other churches, dressing your best on Sunday meant taking every available measure to make yourself look as beautiful as possible. So during those seasons, she would strive to learn the trending makeup and latest hairstyles, using hair products, cosmetics, jewelry, and any other measure available to women of the secular world. The message itself seemed to change from one assembly to another as well, and sometimes *within* the same congregation. (During one of our final read-throughs of this book, Donna reminded me that when she was about fifteen years old, she was approached by a woman at church who told her she should wear makeup and dress in a more grown-up fashion so she would "look her best for God." The next Sunday when she arrived with cosmetics on, another woman from the same group of attendees took her aside and told her it didn't look appropriate.) This was the roller-coaster my mother traversed. After leaving one church in particular that allowed no modern indulgences where women's appearance was concerned, we moved to a more contemporary community. This was one of the sweetest congregations we ever belonged to, where a kind-hearted and well-meaning group of women—upon seeing my mom's wardrobe—quickly pooled their money and bought some new, "more updated" apparel so she would feel more glamourous.

Now, to be clear: Mom was in no way wishy-washy about her beliefs or doctrinal boundaries. Her ability to go bare-faced in one church and then to "glam out" in another doesn't mean her personal opinions shifted as rapidly as the world around her. Rather, she understood that, as a pastor's wife, her ability to blend with and reflect the needs of the current congregation would add significant cohesion to Dad's ministry. This was an era wherein considerable thought, doctrine, and preaching were afforded to the myriad issues that can become stumbling blocks (see Romans 14). She had long since decided that what she cared about *more* than whether she wore makeup was whether she and Dad had an effective ministry. Thus, she strove to find the same balance that Paul found when he discussed being all things to all people (1 Corinthians 9:22). More than anything, she wanted to be effective for the Kingdom.

Yet, in the privacy of our home, there were many times that I watched my mom fix her hair or choose an outfit, then stand in front of the mirror gazing critically at her reflection. I remember saying things like, "Mom, you look pretty." Often her answer was, "Thanks Althia [my given name], but I don't really look like *me*." At that age, I didn't fully understand what she meant, but as I watched her enter subsequent phases of her life, I recognized the conundrum she was feeling at those moments. She knew who she was, and she didn't fully feel as though she had arrived at her end-game destination in ministry. Yet, she knew she was where she was—for that time—called to be. She didn't really fit in, but she was comfortable knowing that she was being obedient…as though following a trail of bread crumbs.

Those around my mother were unaware of her "misfit" status, but it was there, beneath layers of determined submission to the path God had my parents on. But, looking back, I recall the times when that farm girl stood in front of a mirror reflecting the expected suit-and-high-heels look all the other ministers' wives were wearing. Because she was focused on the success of my parents' ministry, the disconnect she felt between her identity and her ministry was nagging, but never destructive.

However, anyone who has read *No Fences: It Started with a Plastic Pony* or *The Boy from El Mirage* (my father's book) will quickly know that their years of faithful service in these avenues eventually led to the founding of Defender Publishing, followed by Skywatch TV and eventually Whispering Ponies Ranch. And, if you've read those books, you'll also know that when my mother finally got her horses as a young adult, after a lifelong desire to have some, she sold them to pay the first month's rent when she and Dad got married. During all those years in ministry, she dreamed of one day having a farm and some horses again. And, of course, this dream came true. But it was years of faithful service to God in other capacities that pushed her beyond her comfort zone and taught her many lessons that transformed her dream of having a farm with horses into one of using that dream for ministry. Operating outside her comfort zone in diligent obedience changed the "someday I want" to "I have been called."

And, here's the best part. By the time the dream of having a pony ranch was realized, the farm girl inside Mom—her *true* identity—had also grown into a seasoned minister, with decades of experience in women's and children's ministry. This refocused the direction of her vision from "hobby farm" to "therapeutic pony farm where traumatized children meet the love of Jesus."

This is where it's vital to differentiate between doing what your hands find to do and making sure your hands find what they are meant to do. Our lives have a season for each, and without the balance of both, we can never reach our true, God-ordained potential. If each of us knew our end-game calling, we would skip all the strange, unplanned encounters and uncomfortable lessons that ultimately prepare us for that calling. Yet, if we don't watch for the ways our dreams and our practical workloads come together, we may become so preoccupied with busywork that we confuse our life chapter with our calling. For many, this means going through periods when, for reasons we may not even be able to put a finger on, we simply feel that we do not fit in. During these times, it is vital that we prayerfully and patiently obey, knowing that more will come.

"I Don't Want to Make Toys!" Hermey the Elf

While Hermey the Elf wasn't a toy in the *Rudolph* movie, he *was* a misfit. Imagine an elf living on the North Pole who, instead of wanting to make Christmas gifts for children, wants to be a dentist.

As we'll discuss in an upcoming chapter, ministerial roles often become typecast into predetermined categories. Then, those who don't fit those roles often feel excluded or isolated, or they become confused about whether they've been called in the first place. (On that note, to clarify: *All* Christians have been called! See Matthew 28:19–20.) Sometimes, either as a result of this confusion or the inability to discern specifically what is it we are called *to do*, we pour ourselves into the nearest job, merely because it's where we find ourselves. Having made a case for the validity in a season of obedience, we will certainly do nothing to discourage people from going about this busywork. After all, it is this busywork that makes up a great part of our earthly contributions to Kingdom work. And, it is certainly better to operate on behalf of heaven at nearly any level than to develop a lackadaisical attitude and sit idly. The thing is, much greater fulfillment and more unique and lasting fruit can be gleaned from finding our true fit. By using our God–given talents and abilities, we end up with more diverse and dynamic forms of ministry.

Part 3: Stepping Off the Island

Over the years, I've seen many folks mistake their life chapter for one of calling. This can have strange and unexpected negative outcomes. For example, I've watched many parents whose "calling" is whatever stage of ministry that's involved with their own children at any particular time. For many women, this means they serve in the church nursery early on, after which they might graduate to teaching the toddlers class and eventually the primaries. You see where I'm going with this, don't you? Men may serve in boys' clubs, youth ministries, and so on. Each of these people is following the calling to be a good parent. And, because this is the ministry that their children are receiving, it makes sense that they would feel the need to contribute in return. But this is different than the call that is separate from others in a person's life: one that is unique and exists between themselves and God. Many times, through a season of obedience—often that service provided by devoted parents in ministry—one's individual destiny surfaces. However, it is vital not to confuse the two. Those whose "calling" follows the path of their own children's progression through church ministries might one day find themselves with both an empty nest *and* an empty-classroom syndrome, saying, "Well, God...*now* what?" Such loss, for parents who have so intricately intertwined their calling with their children's lives, can leave them jarred both personally and ministerially, because they've focused their service upon their kids' needs and not on their own areas of strength.

Recall that, all the time he was building toys, Hermey was aware that his calling was not toy-making; he *just knew* that dentistry was his passion. And he continually advocated for this. For those who struggle to see the difference between obedience and destiny, it is often a conundrum that lands them in a state of burnout. They've hulked up in determination so many times that they become uninspired, unenergetic, unimpassioned, and un- nearly everything else that it takes to do the same—often thankless—job, day in and day out.

If the work you're doing has made you tired and wishing for a break, pray about it. Perhaps respite is just what you need. Or, maybe there's more to it than that. It could be that you simply *must* continue because you are in a season of obedience. If this is the case, God will give you confirmation and strength. If your feelings are as they are because God is ultimately leading you to another path, pray about this as well. Find others whose godly feedback you trust, and seek counsel. Unfortunately, ministerial burnout often comes about as a result of certain (usually difficult, tedious, or seemingly unrewarding) jobs that simply don't draw many volunteers. Thus, those who take them on often feel trapped in them, thinking no one will step up to replace them should they take a sabbatical. Pray about this as well, and discuss it with trusted peers. If God is leading you away from a job He wants continued, He'll bring another laborer.

Most importantly, pray for God to reveal the calling on your life, while paying close attention to your own emerging interests, passions, strengths, and abilities. And, it's important to note, some of these strengths may take our service out of the institution of religion and into our communities. A person can shine the light of God's love to our lost world in many places that fall outside the walls of the church. Think about the opportunities for service in civic buildings, community areas, schools, Big Brother and Big Sister programs, and community parks, not to mention the everyday interactions you have at work or in your neighborhood. These are all areas we can fulfill our calling.

Finding this path doesn't look the same for everyone. Some get started in one direction of ministry and soon discover a series of unique and unexpected doors opening into a place they never expected. Others take on one form of ministry that they serve in for their entire lives. The important thing is to surrender in obedience, doing what you find, while simultaneously and prayerfully asking God to reveal a personalized plan that follows your own strengths and talents.

The Power of Staying: The Square-Wheeled Caboose

One toy that could render several potential parallels in today's society is the train whose caboose has square wheels. For example, there are many people who want to go places but somehow feel held back. For some, there is some sort of disability (whether real or perceived) that they feel limits them. Others may feel weighted down by a painful past, which seems to stop them in their tracks. (We'll address these issues in a bit.)

For our purposes, we look to correlate this misfit toy with a different kind of individual—the one who is called to *stay*. The very concept may be new to some readers, and for some, the limiting insinuation may even be off-putting. Yet, these people are the anchors that keep so many other things grounded to a solid foundation. They are those whose contributions are sometimes overlooked or underappreciated, even by they themselves. It seems that we live in a world that gives large amounts of credit to those we recognize as being on the front lines. In any type of ministry, it's natural for those operating as the mouthpiece to be the most identifiable with the ministry. Yet, these leaders do not—*usually cannot*—act alone. Nor should they. All outreach efforts need numbers of support workers. Furthermore, there are practical aspects to consider as we look back to our misfit toy, the train: In a train, not every car can be at the front. Consider this: If each Christian was the leader of his or her own train, the entire Kingdom of God would be running in different directions. How many of these cross-running trains would collide or jump the tracks?

For each area of ministry, a solid support system of unseen anchor-cabooses is necessary to ensure success. And, these often unsung, behind-the-scenes types are vital, because not only do their efforts add the substance of great infrastructure to an already-great plan, but also because they're the ones who can stop a runaway train.

Those whose calling is found in support roles, fulfilling unrecognized jobs, or otherwise working outside the limelight can often fall into the trap of underestimating the value of their contribution. These individuals of inestimable worth are the people who copy coloring sheets for the children's vacation Bible school classes, wash the dishes in the kitchen after an award or ordination banquet, and keep the church van running so neighborhood children can be brought to Sunday school and other events. They are the unseen workers who clean the church building on Thursday so that visitors feel secure and safe bringing their children to the nurseries and classrooms on Sunday. These are the moms making casseroles to send to bereaved families, the elderly men and women on their knees in a prayer closet at home while younger church members are on mission trips to build facilities for orphans. They're those who painstakingly collect the entire congregation's contact information so that prayer-chain communication throughout the week is possible. They're unsung but reliable contributors who give tithes and offerings like clockwork so that course materials can be purchased, building repairs can be made, and food pantries can be stocked.

These people aren't out doing what many might call "big things." Many will never crisscross the globe, "winning the world for Jesus," because they are daily *reaching* the world around themselves for Him.

Being called to stay can feel like a thankless and anonymous designation. This is sometimes compounded when those at the frontlines forget to thank the quiet contributors who make all forms of ministry possible through their own commitment and even personal sacrifice. (Or, it is likewise compounded when that "thank you" is ill-timed. I can't count how many times I've seen workers publicly thanked via applause in a large assembly, but they missed it, because they were *still* in a back room somewhere, serving and working. The irony...)

If this worker is you, understand that it is *your* contribution that provides the essence of ministry. You may feel that your impact is small because it goes unannounced, but God sees every selfless move you make, even when others do not (Matthew 6:4), and He honors the treasure you lay up in heaven (Matthew 6:19–21). Furthermore, you may never receive all the worldly applause and accolades that you deserve, but you will not be shortchanged your reward in heaven (Matthew 5:12).

There will be souls in heaven as a result of what you do.

Trouble-Targeting, Jelly-Shooting Squirt Gun

A squirt gun shooting anything besides water is silly, right? Well, undoubtedly that's why this malfunctioning toy made the list of "misfits" in the original *Rudolph* movie. Yet, we can make a viable comparison between this anomaly and some of the personalities we see in the world today.

Consider, as an example, a group of people planning a big fundraiser in which the local church will sell food items to raise money for missions. At the planning meeting, most people are comparable to squirt guns that shoot water. The ideas are flowing, creative juices are moving, smiles and excitement circle the room.

Then, in walks *that one guy…*

You know who I'm talking about. He's the "Yeah, but what if…?" guy.

Immediately, *he's* the one who wants to make sure adequate insurance binders are in place to protect the church from liability. *He's* the one who points out that the last time there was a food fundraiser, nobody remembered plastic forks, and it was embarrassing. *He's* the guy who wants to discuss county food-handling regulations so that nobody participating in the fundraiser gets sick from eating food prepared in private kitchens. In fact, *he's* the guy who wants to make sure local authorities are okay with fundraisers that sell food made in people's private kitchens. *He's* the one who wants to label all foods with ingredients for those who may have food allergies.

He's that guy.

What a buzz kill (can I say "buzz kill"?). Just when everybody is having fun and planning what probably will be a successful, "everything-works-out-okay-in-the-end" event, *he* comes in with all the "what ifs" that often seem to unnecessarily overcomplicate matters. He sprays a sticky, heavy, inconvenient truth, yet anybody who's ever been involved in creating policies or bureaucratic infrastructures understands that such proactive brainstorming is not only preventative, but prudent. In an age when ministries suffer continual attack, those who are able to foresee and predict potential issues, liability, or backlash are usually very valuable at keeping church functions cohesive with the outside community.

Certainly these people have become more recognizable for their vitality to operations during the COVID-19 shutdowns. These are the policymakers, the writers of safety procedures, the inspectors, the guardians, and the watchers. These are often the ones who observe subtle nuances to piece together larger scenarios, such as noticing signs of abuse, sensing marital problems, or even anticipating ministerial burnout amongst their peers. Then, in their same "what if" style, they begin to investigate, and often can bring troubles to light before they escalate. Unfortunately, these folks are, at times, ostracized when people want to quickly throw a project or event together without worrying about all the potential problems. For this reason, these troubleshooters often feel rejected, but it's important to understand that it's not actually they themselves who are rejected, but rather the voice of wisdom (Proverbs 23:9) that's viewed with wary eyes. If you have, in your circle of resources, one of these "what if" people who seems to spray a sticky, untimely truth all over the room, give them audience. They're often underappreciated until they're needed, at which point everybody realizes the value of their contribution. For every event or function that comes off without a hitch, it's usually thanks to the forethought of these folks who insist that ideas be padded not only with ingenuity, but with practicality.

It is true that jelly is heavier than water, stickier to deal with, and hard to clean up. But, these "jelly-shooting squirt guns" add vital substance and protection to what might otherwise be projects and plans left vulnerable to problems.

Pushing the Envelope: The Ostrich-Riding Cowboy

The cowboy riding an ostrich we see on the Island of Misfit Toys is an unexpected sight indeed. After all, cowboys are supposed to ride *horses*, right? This very line of thinking is precisely where some of our troubles come in when dealing with people in ministry. After all, we are creatures of habit. If something has always been a particular way, then obviously, it needs to *continue* to be that way.

Yet, we live in times of constant change. And unfortunately, as the outside world has evolved, some of the infrastructure of the church has struggled to keep up, causing congregations to dwindle and bringing questions of relevance to the surface. (Before you become defensive, please understand that I'm not about to say that we need to modernize or "upgrade" our doctrine to make it palatable to today's society. When it comes to change, some things aren't up for grabs. In fact, quite the contrary: In a world where everything is shifting, we need God's immutable truth now more than ever.)

The kind of resistance to conversion I'm referring to occurs in tandem with people and their comfort zones. I've witnessed many churches dividing over the simplest deviations from process. A few examples are:

"That's not how we did it when Pastor Steve was here!"

"I don't like the new schedule."

(Or, my personal favorite…)

"Hey, that's *my* pew! I sit right there every week!"

This opposition to change can manifest in many ways. Sometimes a younger pastor or youth leader comes in, and the older crowd struggles to accept his "newfangled" ideas about using modern tools of technology in conjunction with ministry. Perhaps new songs are introduced that the older crowd finds off-putting. Making changes in curriculum, schedules, or other processes can cause skirmishes amongst those who aren't comfortable with these modifications. Some even become frustrated by fresh methods of drawing youngsters into church.

For example, I knew one youth pastor who gave donuts to the teenagers who attended church on Sunday mornings. This went over pretty well with the younger crowd, and attendance was growing. But, some of the elderly people in the congregation got upset, accusing the minister of "bribing" kids to come to church. (Seriously, the guy took a real verbal beating for this maneuver.)

There's a complication faced by modern-day churches (I studied this at length while writing *The Millennials Paradox*). We live in a world where attending church—and, unfortunately, serving God—is no longer a priority of most people in society. Unfortunately, our culture's mentality separates the notion of being a good citizen from being God-fearing, church-going folk, unlike yesteryear. In fact, only approximately 10 percent of the American population holds a biblical worldview.[46] This means that, for much of the secular world, only two things will bring people into religious assemblies: an appealing incentive or a personal loss that finds them at the end of their rope, broken beyond what they alone are able to repair and finding their way to church in search of relief from this pain. While the second is a novel reason to come to church—and is usually the beginning of a very good testimony—the prerequisite of such a state is a broken and damaged life, and it's also contingent on the hope that people actually find their way to church rather than turning to other, more damaging solutions, further deepening the trouble and pain. Obviously, if we can avoid the second scenario by administering the first strategy preemptively, many of us are all in.

It's an unfortunate fact that some people who *claim* they want their church to grow truthfully do not. It's not that they consciously want others to miss out on the opportunity to obtain salvation, but having their religious safety zone infiltrated by a bunch of "non-Christians" makes them uncomfortable. So, they say with their mouths that they would like to see the church grow, but the instant someone new walks into the building, they get a stare-down. Sure, we all want the lost to find Jesus, but we're not sure we want the "lost" from our community mingling with our "found." Or, perhaps members of our church also serve as our circle of friends, which sounds perfect—until new people come in, interrupting that social chemistry. Maybe the rejection is less intentionally cruel than all of that; perhaps we start noticing what we might consider "shady" characters attending church, and our watchful eyes begin to cause concern for the safety of our children. This is a legitimate worry! (By the way, if you're struggling to figure out how to balance protecting congregants with the influx of new, unknown-and-therefore-not-yet-trusted attendees, this is where those with a "jelly-squirting" personality can be a good resource.)

So, how does all of this relate to a cowboy who doesn't ride a horse? The parallel is simple: We're going to have to begin allowing God to use whatever vehicle He chooses in order to bring people into His kingdom. We may, with laser-focused idealism, think that God is going to keep clean lines between demographics in all these proceedings. We assume He will take all the homeless folks down to the shelter or food bank and reach them there. We may graciously give God our permission to take all the substance abusers down to the rehab center and reach them there. I'm sure we all have some nice woman in mind whom we have preselected to carry on the single-mom ministries of our communities, and so on. (Again, we tend to typecast ministries by personality or appearance, don't we?)

But God may have other plans. And if we are truly about doing His work and reaching people for the kingdom of God, we have to let go of the vehicle *we* think He should use in order to get there, and instead get ready to climb aboard any vehicle He tells us we should be taking.

It Takes a Team: The Boat That Won't Float

Whether or not we realize it, the little sinking boat on the Island of Misfits parallels each one of us. We all have grand places to sail to, yet we need others to hold us up. Without the support of those around us, each of us is likely to sink at times. The concept is really very simple and thus needs no elaboration here. It is scriptural that within the Body of Christ we need to support each other (Galatians 6:2), gather together (Hebrews 10:25), and even look out for one another by lovingly providing guidance (Proverbs 9:8). It has been said many times that no one is an island unto himself or herself. Even Jesus surrounded Himself with people who would help Him during His ministry years. The disciples performed practical tasks, supported Him, prayed with Him, and loved Him. Camaraderie is an innate need held by all of mankind, and those of us who isolate ourselves from others live with unnecessarily difficulty. This simple, sinking boat reinforces this point for all of us.

Nesting Dolls with a Surprise Center

For me, the most obvious parallel for this odd Misfit Island toy—a set of nesting dolls with a wind-up mouse at its center—is to compare it to people who keep up one appearance on the outside, but have another identity hidden beneath many complex, protective layers. At first, readers may assume that I'm referring to people who are hypocritical or "fake." While this could be one explanation, it's not always as simple as that. I'll pick on myself in this example. In my position at Skywatch TV, which frequently requires me to appear publicly, I often appear to be confident and comfortable in front of a crowd or a camera. Yet, many are unaware that I'm an extreme introvert. When I have to talk in front of people, appear in a broadcast, or even do a radio interview over telephone from the comfort of my own home, I experience extreme anxiety. I *never* make any kind of an appearance without first getting completely slammed with stage fright. I mean, I get the works: shortness of breath; trembling throughout my body, especially in my fingers; brain fog; and sometimes even lightheadedness. There's not one interview I participate in that isn't completed by the grace of God. People assume that I'm used to it, and thus conclude that I must be at ease. Inside, however, I feel every bit as awkward as a wind-up mouse—a silly, even stinky, rodent who, under layers of the right clothing and hours spent in preparation, attempts to navigate every public appearance. And, within my mind, each interview or presentation is its own, individual event. Many might think that each book or other written work is its own series of events that can be prepared for simultaneously, but this isn't true. For example, if I were to write a book on the subject of the Holy Spirit, I would not then be prepared to give a series of interviews on that topic just because of the research I did in writing that particular book. Even after the book is in print, the subsequent season of promotional interviews becomes a period of continued research on that particular topic. Nor could I sit down and prepare for "all the interviews about the Holy Spirit," at the same time, because each interviewer often has different questions they want to ask, a unique audience who may have varying points of interest, or other reasons that each interaction must be prepared for. After each one, I'm exhausted, and must take time to rest, recuperate, and then restudy to prepare for the next one. And, for me, each successful interview is its own milestone after which I must return to my study desk and "wind up" again.

Perhaps you sometimes feel this way: Under the heading of being a positive influence, a good example, or even to cast positive light on your ministerial efforts, you keep a charismatic, upbeat, energetic or magnanimous outer shell, but inside, perhaps everything you do wears you out. Maybe each milestone is taken in slices, between which you must recuperate. Perhaps you've grown "weary in well doing" (Galatians 6:9). Or, perhaps you're one who has spoken too much good, old-fashioned truth for the itching ears around you, and your listeners or readers have now distanced themselves from you. Could you be struggling with burnout, but for the sake of being a force for good, you've continued to keep up the appearance that you're not worn out or discouraged?

If this is you (and it is *all* of us at some point, especially for those of us in ministry and service), allow me to encourage you: Your inner mouse has a wind-up crank for a reason. Notice also that a wind-up toy doesn't go very far before it needs to be cranked again. We are not battery-operated. We don't have the ability to put an Energizer or a Duracell in our pack and continue on for five additional years with no need for rest. Any wind-up will need to be re-cranked on the same day as its use. Don't be afraid to take a break, find rest, surround yourself with encouraging people, and prioritize your own needs sometimes. Assuming that self-care is selfish is an easy trap to fall into, but it's a false statement.

If you're in ministry, if you work, if you're raising a family, or if you're generally participating in life on nearly any level, there is no way around prioritizing your own needs every now and then. I've mentioned before that, growing up in church, one sees a lot of the behind-the-scenes troubles experienced by those within ministry, and I can say with authority that burnout is a very real threat. Often, under the heading of having a "servant's heart," we push ourselves past the breaking point, but nobody can operate like that forever. Even Jesus took opportunities at different times in His ministry to withdraw and recuperate. If you are secretly tired and wishing for a break, but you fear no one will step up and carry the load you shoulder while you rest, pray about it. God will place the burden on someone else if He wants that work to continue, or He will provide another way for you to find the rest you need.

When Bears...Fly? The Winged Bear

For many, this nonsensical hybrid of bear and bird is silly and would certainly be considered an outcast toy. Yet, what are the implications of this combination? First of all, we see a bear: a mighty, formidable image of strength and hardiness; a creature that's not easily intimidated. Bears are guardians, and they're resilient. Yet they also symbolize a type of gentleness framed within their unmovable power. That, on its own, is worthy of respect. But I'd like to take the metaphor a step further. And, while many of our comparisons to misfit toys have leaned more toward messages to women, I want to take this opportunity to talk more directly to men.

I've known many "gentle giant" types in church who provided loving, male mentorship for both children and peers who had no other such iconic individuals in their lives. Often, these men don't hold the official title of "minister," per se, but their presence enriches the lives of those around them in ways they cannot imagine. In particular, I can recall many men who work full-time in secular realms and juggle many responsibilities that keep them from being involved in church full-time, but they still make it a point to do what they can, sacrificing evenings, weekends, and other luxuries to ensure that a generation of fatherless children gets to see a model of godly men in action. (Statistics say that from nineteen to twenty-four million children are presently growing up without a father figure in the home).

In an era when so many young men are being raised to believe that manliness is toxic, their own masculine attributes fall under attack when they're around the same age that the absence of a strong male role model leaves them most vulnerable: the pre-teen to teenaged years. The societal pressure to deny their masculine traits leaves an entire generation of young men conflicted at their very core, and many desperately need strong but gentle models of what being a man is *truly* all about. The men who prioritize making time to reach out, working with children and teens who desperately need this type of influence in their lives, make a difference that can scarcely be put into words—and certainly one that can't be measured.

If you're a man who has been mentoring children or teens, please understand that your impact cannot be measured. You are *so desperately needed* right now, to stand up and be a solid role model. (Note: If you've been beating yourself up because other responsibilities keep you from being more involved in ministry, please don't. Give yourself grace and simply try to be as active as you can.) As a provider, you truly carry a large load of responsibilities. Every moment you're able to give as a mentor is a gift that will impact the Kingdom in ways that can never be counted in this lifetime.

Perhaps you've taken for granted your influence on those around you. It's easy to underestimate one's value in the lives of those who look up to them. After all, most people who gain clout in the eyes of others don't set out with this mission in mind; it simply happens as one's character is revealed over time. On the other hand, those who *do* intentionally attempt to accomplish such ends often have ulterior motives, which are usually detected by some and thus fosters a sense of mistrust. In this way, it is often the pure at heart who, without even meaning to, land in the position of preferred role model and mentor.

Because of this, some of the most profound influencers are often people who are completely unaware of the depth of their esteem in the eyes of others. These "teddy-bear types" are frequently mild-mannered and gentle, yet tough and resilient. My point is that it could be *you* who has become this symbol for many younger men who are looking to you for an example of tender but firm, nontoxic masculinity. And, if you are one of the last people that you may have suspected would land in such a role—or if you were never looking for such esteem—it may be for *this very reason* that you are the first person that these young ones look to.

So what of the bear's wings? That's the last physical attribute we would imagine on a big, burly bear. Surely, there is some mistake.

No, not at all! For every strong individual who has put the needs of others first; who has modeled kind and caring power for a generation of fatherless children; who has wiped the tears of a child with strong, calloused, and work-worn hands: You may think that your role is small. Perhaps you don't "preach," "teach," or in some other way stand in front of the crowd and address the masses, but understand that you will soar with the eagles; you are meant for great heights, because you have practiced what God Himself calls *pure, undefiled* religion (James 1:27). You are influencing an entire generation for the Kingdom of heaven! You may see yourself—in your own mind's system of ministerial hierarchy—as the guy at the bottom of the totem pole, but you achieve a higher level of purity in your service to God than you can ever imagine.

Digging Deeper: Yukon Cornelius

An interesting fact about prospector Cornelius in the *Rudolph* movie that has been mentioned already is the fact that he continually licks his pickax. Many viewers don't know why he does this. We won't linger long on this subject, as it ties into the things we'll say next regarding the Abominable Snowman, but we will take a minute to point out that sometimes people do things for reasons we don't understand. At times, the motivations for other people's behaviors aren't only enigmatic, but sometimes the behavior is so off-putting that we struggle to even care what makes these people tick. Yet, if we understood what drives their actions, it's very likely we would view their conduct much differently—and perhaps with more grace. Prospector Cornelius' compulsive pickax-licking habit makes perfect sense once we realize that he is mining for peppermint. In the same way, the behaviors of those around us can become clearer when we take the time to understand their motivation.

Beauty in the Beast: The Abominable Snowman

The abominable snowman was for some time a villain in the *Rudolph* story. However, when Hermey the elf pulled the monster's teeth, he became nice. Essentially, disarming the creature began a transformation whereupon the formidable creature became a gentle giant. Even though he wasn't a resident of the Island of Misfit Toys and wasn't officially a misfit, this certainly deserves a place within our profiles here. It's no secret that many people are vastly misunderstood or are even intentionally mean. Sometimes they're carrying so much responsibility that they don't feel they have time for "niceties," or they have such hidden pain that they've learned to preemptively attack before others have the chance to target them. They may be grumpy, angry, hurtful, etc., but often are in a great amount of discomfort; disarming the situation can give them an opportunity to reinvent themselves. For most people, combat is a means of survival, but not a preferred state of interaction. Often, if we can find a way to defuse a person's conflict mode, we'll find they're capable of becoming friendly. (And, once this transformation is complete, they can be some of the most loyal and defensive allies we can have!) This can occur under multitudes of situations in church, but one particular example comes to mind more than others.

I will call the little boy "Michael." He was probably about eight years old when he began riding the church bus to our services occasionally. The fact that he didn't come very often, for some of the teachers, was a confessed relief. You probably know the type of kid I'm referring to when I describe Michael: He was hyperactive, didn't follow directions, behaved loudly, picked on the other kids, wouldn't listen to the Bible stories, and insisted on sprinting in the hallways despite continually being told not to run. One fall, we decided to begin planning a Christmas program with our children's church program. The kids were given several songs to sing as a group. Early on in our rehearsals, their voices were shy, quiet, and unenthusiastic.

Anyone who has known my mom for very long knows that she has a way of seeing the best in people. When she looked at Michael, she didn't see a constantly-in-trouble kid or feel relieved when he wasn't there. Instead, she saw a hurting child who had been treated poorly by most of the world. She saw his antics as outcries for love and attention.

And, in her typical form, she bypassed any temptation to be hard on him, instead channeling her energy into building him up. "Michael," she would say, "you sing beautifully. I had no idea you were so talented!" Then she would address the kids around him by saying things like, "Hey everybody, try to be really smiley and energetic, the way Michael is when he sings." This and many other compliments spilled from my mom's lips the entire time she was in the room with him.

But don't think for a second that Michael didn't test Mom, because he did. At one point he became so out of control that he jumped on my brother Joe's back and physically attacked him, and *bit* him on the shoulder! Needless to say, there were times that reprimands were necessary. But when she had to correct him, my mother always said something like this: "Now, Michael, I *know* you're capable of doing better than this. You're such a good kid! I've seen it in your eyes *and* in your heart. I know that you're here because you want to make Jesus proud and you want to do a good job. And, *you are* doing a good job, except I need you to make this one adjustment to your behavior."

She would then briefly identify the out-of-line conduct and explain the specific change that she needed to see. He responded positively every time. It was interesting to watch, because many in the church had tried a firmer, more intimidating approach, which never seemed to phase Michael at all. Mom's loving, respectful, and clear communication sandwiched reinforcement, acceptance, and forgiveness into a message that the boy responded to. By the time the Christmas program took place, no child was singing more loudly or beaming more brightly than Michael.

And guess what else?

Somewhere along the way, during preparations for the play, Michael had started bringing his siblings with him to church. On the night of the actual presentation, his mom came. A few weeks later, she came again. And then again. And then again. Five years later, his entire family was attending church, including his dad!

While I am not singlehandedly crediting my mother for this entire family's transformation, I do know that she was instrumental in sowing seeds of change within the boy, which later extended to the household. The revolution began by one person exercising patience to a child who had the very real ability to rub people wrong. Yet, as each of his family members not only began to attend church, but—more importantly—gave their lives to Christ, a single generation changed directions for this entire family tree. This is the fruit that comes from being able to recognize someone who has a type of pain that makes them abrasive or difficult to get along with, and the willingness to work beyond that barricade.

It goes without saying that many people who come to church do so because they are experiencing pain and seeking relief. If we believers really mean it when we say we want to reach people for the Kingdom of heaven and we want to see our churches grow, then we have to be willing to look for the deeper motivations behind why people act the way they do. And, when God gives us wisdom regarding how to react, we must be willing to take the high road and respond in a way that heals.

Loving Ally: King Moonracer

This character—a majestic and fierce, but gentle, winged lion—in our 1964 film is the master of the Island of Misfit Toys. Not only does he care deeply for all the outcasts who live in his care, but he spends each night flying about the entire world, seeking out any other lost and lonely toys. Upon finding these exiles, he brings them to the island, offering them a home, camaraderie, and a destiny beyond isolation. Just as he searches for these playthings, he likewise tries to find children who will love and play with each toy. Once he has located such a home, he then delivers the toy to its new home.

I know what you may be thinking: *This sounds like Someone else I know of.* An Advocate who, out of love and compassion, seeks out the lost and hurting and redeems them into a new life of belonging and hope. If this is the conclusion you leaped to, then—spoiler alert—allow us to inform you that you are correct. King Moonracer obviously symbolizes the Lion of Judah (we might also compare him to Aslan of the C. S. Lewis series, *The Chronicles of Narnia*). Ultimately, King Moonracer is a fitting representation of Jesus the Savior: He's the Defender of the helpless, the Life-Giver to the dying, the Friend to the forgotten, and the Champion of the outcast.

King Moonracer is an iconic character because he epitomizes someone who exists to extend hope to those without it, those who have been so abandoned, isolated, and forgotten that they have no place to call home.

The guardianship, advocacy, and interpersonal connection that this lion offers in conjunction with his active seeking-out of the banished is reminiscent of God's endless pursuit of lost souls. And, when he finds these outcasts, there is no criteria they must fulfill, no limit beyond which they become "too damaged" or "too quirky" to join the other misfits. Instead, their very status as oddballs qualifies them for a place in this family. It is Moonracer's desire that all toys have a place to belong, and that they live happy and fulfilled lives where they can exchange joy with one another and the children.

In Luke 15, we read of multiple examples of the same type of redemptive searching that is characteristic of Moonracer. Verses 4–7, for example, explain that a shepherd who lost a single sheep out of a flock of one hundred would certainly leave the remaining ninety-nine to look for the missing one. Furthermore, it is stated that all of heaven celebrates over the return of the missing one. And verses 8–10 describe a woman's diligent search throughout her entire house for one coin lost from her ten. Again, we are told that heaven rejoices over the reappearance of the mislaid.

In the parable of the prodigal son, which we read in the remainder of Luke 15 (verses 11–32), a young man asks his father to divide his estate and grant him his portion of his inheritance at once, so that he may take it and venture into the world to make a different life for himself. This is in poor taste on several levels. First of all, for a son to ask for his share of an inheritance in hopes of obtaining it from a healthy, *living* father is similar to the son telling this paternal figure that he has grown weary of awaiting his death.[47] Additionally, from the description of the father's assets as referenced throughout the story, we see that he was a man of vast estate, which would have taken some great effort to divide, liquidating his son's portion. In this way, we see that this request was rude, selfish, inconvenient, and something that would have brought embarrassment within the surrounding community. (Resources were not discharged quietly in such communal settings.)[48] Further, inheritances weren't only used to secure future generations' financial security, but they also represented a passing-on of the family business: The younger descendants would carry on the older generation's way of life. To demand that one's percentage be "cashed out" in such a way insulted the entire family on many levels. We can now imagine how much worse this atrocity became when the wayward son squandered this allotment on "riotous living" (verse 13), which many scholars sum up in such terminology as "parties and prostitutes" (based on insinuations in verse 30). At such a time, a son would be considered such a disgrace that he would be deemed "dead" to his family, and at the very least would be cut off from his surrounding community.[49]

For the father in this parable, what was asked of him was an affront to him as a paternal figure, as a provider, as a maker of his family heritage, and as a loving child-rearer; it disgraced him before his community. He had every right to deny the request, yet he acquiesced. The story itself describes a father whose unselfishness supersedes that of human ability, paralleling the supernatural love of our Heavenly Father, even in the face of shortsighted, self-seeking, disgraceful rejection placed upon Him by the ones he raised up in the first place.[50] We *should* be outcast from Him. We *deserve* to be isolated. And yet, Luke 15:20 and 32 describe a

Father who is constantly watching from afar for his returning, wayward children: "But when he was yet a great way off, his father saw him, and had compassion, and ran, and fell on his neck, and kissed him," and later, announcing, "[my son] was dead [to this family], and is alive again [restored to the status of this family]; and was lost, and is found."

Like the father in the parable of the prodigal son, God is seeking those who have rejected and even disgraced Him, desiring only to see them restored to His family. And, similar to this paternal character, He does not care what we have done or how we may have wasted our inheritance up to now. He will *run* to greet us, just as the elderly man in the story of the prodigal son did. In the same way that King Moonracer searches for the lonely, rejected, and the hurting, the Lord wants to bring the lost ones into a place of belonging. God never intended for mankind to live a life of separation from Him. Nor was the Creator's aim ever that we would reside in isolation from others.

At one point in the *Rudolph* movie, the young, red-nosed exile approaches King Moonracer, asking if he can live permanently on the Island of Misfit Toys since he, too, is an oddball. The king denies the request, saying, "Unlike playthings, a living creature cannot hide himself on an island."[51] The crowned lion immediately follows this refusal up with his own petition, asking Rudolph to help him find children who will love the residents of the island so that they can be rehomed into happy, new lives. What a touching sentiment of advocacy and redemption that, even at that moment, the royal guardian's thoughts are toward beseeching redemption for his beloved residents.

If you are one who has self-isolated because of past pain or trauma, because of feelings of unworthiness or awkwardness, there is a King—King Jesus, the Lion of Judah—who wants you to know you *belong*. Perhaps you are secluded because it is you who has rejected Him. Understand that He wants nothing more than for the missing ones to return. He has clearly stated in His Word that all of heaven rejoices upon the homecoming of *one* prodigal son (or daughter)! There is a place *you* fit in: You are unique, loveable, and beautiful in His eyes. Your flaws, short-comings, vulnerabilities, and weaknesses are a part of your testimony. You are completely redeemable—you're only an outcast if you choose to remain one. He is seeking you out, even now. He will restore you to the status of being a member of His family, and He will place you in a permanent home where you can give and receive joy and love, and experience true peace.

Regardless of why you may have found yourself separated from the Body of Christ, it is time to come home. A family reunion is awaiting you—and, like the father whose wayward son returned to him, God is watching in hopes of your return, ready to embrace you.

5

Growing Up a Misfit

 *By Allie Henson*

One of the questions people ask me repeatedly is what it was like to grow up as the daughter of Tom and Nita Horn. To some degree, the query is connected to this book about misfits, since these two have walked a path and followed a calling that has been so matchless. Other members of this family, likewise, follow a distinctive course and see unusual things. However, many of the people who make this inquiry do so not to look for a commentary on church underworkings or a ministry exposé, but usually more from curiosity regarding the "family side" of Tom and Nita Horn. To satisfy that curiosity, I'll indulge the reader's interest.

When I was under two years old (I have very young memories—in some of them I'm not yet even walking), we were living in a small, two-bedroom trailer on the corner of a local farmer's corn field (this living situation is discussed at length in *The Boy from El Mirage*.) I had a fun world of the simplest playthings to occupy my time: a pavement slab outside with a wading pool on it, a red tricycle, and later, a red-and-white, candy-cane-striped swing set that made me feel like I owned my own peppermint-themed playground.

One day, a box of books came in the mail. My parents were celebrating "Daddy getting his homework in the mail!" Of course, I had no idea at the time that what had arrived were his correspondence textbooks for becoming a trained, licensed, and later, ordained minister. At my age, all of that was far over my head. What I recall vividly was my daddy, despite juggling more than one job, coming home and closing himself into one of the dark, 1970s wood-tone-paneled bedrooms of our trailer between work shifts so that he could study. Mom and I would keep each other company while taking care not to make noise that would distract him; whatever he was up to in there was emphasized as very important. This went on for quite a season—a few years—until one day, another box arrived that was celebrated much the same way as earlier shipment of books. As young as I was, I didn't understand what I was looking at, but I later learned it was his certificate showing he had completed the courses. What I distinctly *did* understand at the time was that, as part of this small merriment, Dad took out a suit catalog he'd been keeping at his desk, and he and mom quickly began pouring over it, discussing colors, cuts, designs, and more. She measured him in a variety of directions: arm length, leg length, shoulder width, etc. Then they wrote the numbers on a card that had been torn out along its perforated edge, placed the card in an envelope with a check, and put it in the mailbox. Several weeks later, the fruits of this labor arrived.

To reward himself for his hard work in finishing ministerial school, and to launch his newfound role with style, my dad had ordered two new suits—both made of polyester, and each featuring pants with a bell-cut leg and a jacket on which every angle of the design took on an exaggerated, curvy swoop. The buttons of the jacket had a pearlescent tone that added a modern, edgy look, causing what may have otherwise been mistaken for a leisure suit to be regarded as completely professional business attire. The best part about these stylish outfits were the colors: One was maroon and the other was hunter green. As my father emerged from the next room to show the first one to my mom, I'll never forget their excitement at seeing this tangible manifestation of the new chapter in their lives. In the wide-eyed excitement of their youthful zeal, they just *knew* God was leading them into a path of service for the Kingdom, and the milestone of purchasing the first two "pastor's suits"—as ridiculously and as quintessentially "1978" as they may have been—was one of the earliest signals that their dream of being in the ministry was unfolding.

So, for your reading enjoyment, there it is: A young, beaming Tom Horn in a hunter green or maroon, polyester, bell-bottomed leisure/ business suit, Bible in hand, ready to take the gospel into the world— with a giddy, barely-older-than-adolescent Nita beside him, grinning ear to ear.

You're welcome.

Yet, these two had no idea what the journey they were about to embark upon would hold. Looking back, I see that the types of obstacles they would face and the predicaments that would surface in churches they led were so unique that their accumulation of experiences carved the unparalleled ministerial path that eventually paved the way for Sky-watch TV, Defender Publishing, and Whispering Ponies Ranch. But anyone who knows much about my parents will remember that neither was raised in church, and each had childhood experiences that rendered them a "misfit" in their own way. This couple who, for years, led congregations and successful ministry, were just a pair of oddballs who answered God's call on their lives at a young age with the brave and obedient words, "Send me."

We're All Misfits Here

Throughout the years of my parents' ministry, I witnessed—as any pastor's child does—many kinds of church situations and personalities. There is one circumstance that I've observed consistently: the ironic and cyclical relationship that many people tend to have with religion. It can occur in the Christian church or within other faith systems, and goes like this:

A flawed and broken person reaches the end of his rope with life's devastation, and turns to some sort of church for intervention. A message of hope is given to this individual, who decides to give faith a try. He subscribes, partly based on the example of the "perfect" lives he sees around him. It's as though the seemingly impeccable people he's surrounded by advertise that he, too, can have a life free of struggle. As he settles into the congregation, one of two things happens. The first is that he does not see the trials, temptations, and other such real-life issues experienced by those around him, so he wonders why he is the only one facing such obstacles when, as far as he can see, he has followed all the guidelines and rules. The other, more common, outcome of this scenario is that, as he becomes more familiar with those he is observing, he realizes that he has joined up with a group of faulty, lacking, damaged, baggage-carrying, sinful, and sometimes hypocritical people who, like himself, never "had it all together," nor were they *ever* free from the cares of life. He may feel duped or disenchanted, depending on how intentional this psychological "bait-and-switch" appears to have been. If he has focused on the membership of the assembly more than on its faith-based objective, he may feel jaded toward religion and leave. If he stays, the emerging differences between all congregants may make him feel as though he doesn't fit in quite the way he thought he did. Either way, there is an ostracizing that takes place and fragments relationships between believers who should be banding together.

This is how Christianity loses a lot of its new converts. First, newcomers often subscribe to the misconception that faith will remove all the problems from their lives. Second, they have a notion that since other Christians appear to have minimal problems, their own life issues must be the result of something they themselves are doing wrong.

Before proceeding, I must say that the second explanation, on occasion, can be true, because our own sinful choices can perpetuate certain struggles in our lives. This is why, when we accept Jesus as Savior, we must also take Him as Lord. In this way, we follow God's guidelines in the hopes that we will identify and shed sinful thoughts and actions that we're allowing to enter our lives by our choices. However, another idea needs be brought to light here: Most who turn to the church for intervention perceive those around them to be perfect, since they often appear to have all the answers. However, churches are full of imperfect people whose lives are filled with struggles that often aren't evident to newcomers. The reasons these struggles are kept hidden are as varied as the individuals themselves.

But the perception to those outside the church is often that the folks within are all enjoying perfect lives, and that there is some sort of sameness across the congregation. It can appear as though Christians all live, think, speak, dress, and act the same way. To those who don't feel as though they fit in, this self-image of being a misfit can become equivalent to feeling as if they don't belong in the Body of Christ. Yet, the irony is that we should never assimilate to be exactly like one another: God made each of us different. No two of us are alike. The Lord's very hand crafted each of us as we were being formed (Psalm 139:13–14). He sees each of us individually and takes a personal interest in us—so much so that even the number of our hairs are counted by Him (Luke 12:7). If we are striving to become the unique people that He fashioned with His own hand, then the longer we work together in His service, the more our beautiful differences and strengths should emerge as we grow in Him. The corporate appearance of sameness is not an image that we should subscribe to, nor should we feel outcast in our individuality.

The perception that we don't fit into the Body of Christ is a deception used to keep us from bonding together in His mission. The truth is that a thriving, vital, fully operational Body of Christ is made up of a congregation of misfits who have found their individual purposes in Him and then have come together as an assembly of spiritually mature mentors who cooperatively work to bring in others and disciple them.

They've embraced their uniqueness—their distinctive talents, strengths, and even their quirks!—and have harnessed these abilities for use in the Kingdom of God. It's a collective of flourishing and matchless people who have found their place in the world and, because of this, they have unparalleled gifts to share, further extending the gospel and the hope of Christ to a lost and dying humanity in ways that are as varied as the people who make up that Body.

And *none* of them is quite the same as another. They are united because they are misfits who have realized that they *belong*.

Before Continuing

Before moving forward, it is necessary to clarify one thing. To state that God made each of us unique and that we are to embrace those differences is not the same as tolerating sin. There are plenty of other resources dedicated to this topic, so we won't dwell on it here, but it is these authors' goals to set individuals free to find and embrace their God-given talents and abilities. Likewise, we wish to encourage them to shed the stigma or insecurity that holds them back, and unleash them to follow that directive. However, it is a tactic of the enemy to cause God-given traits and sinful desires to become confused with one another, and this is a pitfall that can create ambiguity, which makes people latch on to sin under the concept that it is a God-embedded characteristic, since they "feel" a certain way. This is *not* what we are encouraging when we ask that readers embrace their uniqueness.

For example, let's say someone loves to steal. She may naturally be very good at sneaking in and out of buildings unnoticed, and she may have a body language that allows her to slip things into her pockets with ease, whereas others find that their own clumsy movements would get them caught. This person may feel that she has what would appear to be a "natural gift" of thievery, but this doesn't mean her God-ordained calling is to steal. ("Thou shalt not steal"; see Exodus 20:15.) Whether out of perceived material necessity, the boredom of idle hands, lack of positive role models, or any other potential motive, ranging from childhood trauma to unmet psychological needs and spiritual attack, this person has chosen to follow a path that does not align with Scripture. To say she feels the compulsion to swipe things—and is good at it—is *not* to say that God created her to be a thief and that she should embrace the behavior as part of her role in God's Kingdom.

"Inspiration" and Religion: The Cyclical Trap

One day, Donna came into the office we share and told me that she had been given a book assignment that involved highlighting the parallels between the misfit toys of the 1964 *Rudolph* film and modern-day believers. The idea behind the book was most definitely to inspire people to see past their own differences and find a new inspiration in their role within the Body of Christ. (Please note before moving further that this does not always mean in-church ministry; it can take place anywhere that one finds a place to contribute to the world around them and shine the light of a positive Christian witness). On hearing the topic, I smiled supportively, but didn't envy her. (It wasn't until later that I was added as a coauthor.) Having been raised as a pastor's kid, I've seen firsthand the emotional roller-coaster that accompanies the aforementioned cycle of church members who join, but later leave the church, and words such as "inspiration" and "enthusiasm" are always a big part of this process. Over time, I had become jaded about such words. To me, these and similar terms had become labels by which people expressed their initial excitement over nearly any new idea, whether it's social or cultural movements, religious trends, educational programs, etc. But, I've always noticed, that alongside such energy, the joy attached to it that seems to swell during any new phase quickly wears off along with the novelty.

Thus, these terms became almost cheapened in my world—reduced to phrases that could easily be paired with nearly anything falling into the category of "New Year's resolution:"

"I'm *so inspired* about this new diet I'm trying out!"

"I can't wait to get home and start organizing my entire house from floor to ceiling, I'm *so excited* now!"

"I know I can break that bad habit; I'm really *enthusiastic* about it this time."

By now, surely you've gathered that children of ministers grow up seeing both the good and the bad that occur behind the scenes in any type of ministry. This isn't because our parents sit us down and reveal all the details; as ministers, confidentiality is one of their strongest assets. My parents never any shared sensitive or private information with us kids, but children are more perceptive than many people realize, and are always watching. By sheer proximity, the children of ministers have a decent understanding of what takes place.

Thus, the child is witness to those devout ministers who work their fingers to the bone, often filling multiple roles within the church just to keep the doors open. Conversely, these kids also observe cases where hypocrites, repeated backsliders, or ministers who are insincere appear on the scene. But one of the most common elements witnessed are those well-meaning people who restart aspects of their life nearly weekly. It's often an emotional, self-perpetuating cycle, and it works a little like this:

Someone decides to make a certain change within his life. He repents of any wrongdoing, and asks God to strengthen and inspire him moving forward. He may be praying about a new ministry endeavor, to be freed of some sort of continuing sin, or some other request. At some point, he will amass a type of energy that fuels the journey for a time. Inevitably, however, he grows tired and falls into old habits, begins to find the new endeavor tiresome, or he otherwise "loses his inspiration." Then he perceives this slump as God's strength having left. Often, at this point, the object of the initial prayer is abandoned.

Often, after a time of being down on himself for these "failures," he may become inspired again, whether to pursue the same goals he previously prayed for, or to move on to a new objective. When this occurs, the person seems to find new energy, declare new inspiration, and he's off to the races again…

And the cycle continues.

In similar fashion, there are well-meaning people who re-rededicate their lives to Christ nearly every Sunday at the altar. Please understand that I and my cowriters *certainly* are not making light of anybody's spiritual experiences, and every salvation story is a beautiful transition from death to life that is the very reason Jesus suffered on the cross. But for some, the cyclical pattern mentioned before becomes the only way they are able to define their salvation. This means they regard their entire salvation as requiring a weekly restart instead of digging deeper to sustain true spiritual growth. And because they don't find roots wherein they can dig deeper into all that God has for their lives, they equate the tearful, emotional altar experience with the heights of God's intent for them. Thus, when the feelings of "being saved" wear off, so does the determination to follow Christ. This results in converts who repeatedly offer big responses in church, but whose lives demonstrate little or no manifestation of God's boundaries, His doctrines, *or* His victory. And, unfortunately, those watching both scenes play out begin to perceive religion as impotent or the whole thing as fake.

Because this repeat conversion can be perceived as insincerity or the notion that religion doesn't work when applied in practical ways to people's lives, some onlookers decidedly distance themselves from what many believers accept as normal altar activity. Many wonder how much of what they witness really is God manifesting Himself to believers, and how much is well-meaning people seeking an emotional response as tangible reassurance that they're in touch with a Supreme Being in an effort to assuage their own spiritual insecurity. When such questions are accompanied with behind-the-scenes knowledge about the same individual's life, observers' impressions often polarize, creating a sort of "split impression" of the same individual. For example, those who are watching what's taking place at the front of the sanctuary may see someone demonstrating a physically exuberant and passionate response at the altar each Sunday, and simultaneously be aware that the same person is still walking in a sinful lifestyle. As a result, onlookers struggle to process this duality, and some take extreme measures in their own search for answers. The result can be another form of ostracizing within the Body.

My Misfit Story

As a minister's kid, this became an issue for me. I never wondered about my salvation, but I was uncertain of how to reconcile seeing repeated weekly or biweekly conversions that seemed to lack staying power in people's lives. (I later discovered that what was missing in these congregants was that, while they took Jesus as "Savior," they never accepted Him as "Lord.") Similarly, I never forgot the many people in church—even ministers sometimes—who were different people behind the scenes than the righteous, godly individuals they presented themselves to be in front of crowds. In fact, when I was in my early twenties, I rebelled against God for a time, and then rededicated my life to Him. Having watched as so many subscribed to the spiritual rollercoaster their emotions seemed to carry them on, I desired to serve Him from a place rooted in my intellect. This included my will, my actions, and the direction in which I pointed my energy, a place that—for *me*, at least—runs deeper and more disciplined than just my feelings. I wanted my moves to be calculated, purposeful, logical, and fruitful. (This makes sense, as it is how I approach all of my relationships in general, whether it's with colleagues, friends, family, and even my children).

Part 3: Stepping Off the Island

I always fully supported other people who had exuberantly physical or passionate responses in worship of the Lord, but I filtered my interactions through a calculated and intellectual place within my psyche. I am aware that God reaches different people in different ways. And, since He blesses each of us individually and distinctly, our responsive worship manifests differently. Some people dance in the Spirit, some raise their hands and sing, and some laugh or shout exuberantly in the joy of the Lord, while others cry or quietly take to their knees in devout prayer.

With all of this as a preface, my motivation for saying all of these things is to explain that in a room full of Pentecostal, pew-jumping, shouting, singing, and dancing saints, I'm usually the girl at the back who is praying quietly. And, for years, there were some who tried to make me feel as though I was somehow less spiritual than those around me—or worse—farther away from God because my worship did not look like theirs.

There were even some who suggested that I try mimicking the activities of others, in the hope that God would see it as some type of "gesture of faith." Not wishing to subscribe to anything that wasn't authentic, I declined. For that, I was often—or maybe I just *perceived* myself as being—increasingly ostracized from others within the church. There were times I felt disconnected from the Body of Christ and wondered what I was spiritually lacking that made everybody else able to worship with such exuberance but that, for me, seemed only awkward.

Please don't misunderstand what I'm saying. It wasn't an issue of being embarrassed by doing what I saw others doing; that would've been far easier to get over. After all, I'm often in situations that are uncomfortable, and in those cases, I just muster up the courage to do what I have to do. This reservation ran deeper. It was something about the fact that trying to manufacture the physical responses that others experienced came with a sort of warning that I couldn't shake. Even now, I struggle to explain it. I finally decided that if I was being sincere before God and worshiping Him in spirit and in truth (John 4:24), then I had to trust

159

that my honesty before Him was what He wanted most of all. Yet, I still often felt like an oddball in church.

Then, one day several years back, Donna and I attended a ladies' conference. We were going for business-related matters, but several of us prayerfully felt there were underlying reasons God wanted us to attend. From the onset, we received several unexpected, God-ordained confirmations that we should go—even before we left for travel.

A day or two before our departure, however, I began to feel run down; I assumed that the busy-ness of travel preparations and shortened sleeping hours the nights of that week were the culprits. But, by the morning after we arrived at our hotel room, I began suffering symptoms of what I perceived to be a very mean cold. I attributed it to the air-circulation systems on the plane, the changes in time zone, altitude, and climate, and every other adaptation a person's system makes when flying between states. (This was before the COVID-19 outbreak, when most people went about their typical business despite the potential exposure to the virus, so long as the symptoms seemed common enough not to be particularly threatening. Later, I was diagnosed with a sinus infection, bronchitis, and pneumonia, all of which were relatively advanced, since I didn't see a doctor until after returning home.)

As Donna and I arrived at the conference, the first thing we noticed was that, despite the hot temperatures outside, the air-conditioning of the auditorium had been cranked to what must've been a mere four or five degrees. Okay, you may detect my sarcasm, but the truth is that women all around the building were huddled in blankets and shivering. One would think that, at this point, the conference administrators would see what was going on and adjust the temperature, but it remained that cool for the duration of the meetings. Additionally, this was a very charismatic event offering every physical avenue of praise I had ever known of, and a few I had never seen before. During song services, some people danced with tambourines or waved flags and other colorful cloths through the air, while others blew shofars, clapped, laughed, or shouted. Most activity of this nature occurred toward the front of the auditorium directly below the stage, where many worshipers gathered to praise during the singing.

The song services themselves were conducted much like rock-n-roll concerts. There were fog machines, laser lights, and a full band with every kind of modern instrument one could imagine. There was a man whom they had brought in as a special guest called a "kinetic worship leader." In all my Pentecostal experiences, I had never seen anything quite like this. I didn't want judge other people's methods of praising God, but I found it odd that, at a ladies' conference, a reasonably attractive man would be stationed to dance on stage in front of the female audience. (At one point, Donna even overheard the woman seated in front of us describe the man as being "hot.") Part of his presentation was to wave flags and other colorful equipment through the air—some of which displayed pictures of religious icons such as praying hands, the Star of David, the Lion of Judah, the cross, a dove representing the Holy Spirit, and other easily recognizable elements found in Scripture. However, many of the man's moves seemed as though they were a modified form of belly dancing, complete with the rolling hip and shoulder motions. I found it strange that the display was brought into a religious setting where many women were single, and where others had traveled away from their husbands for the week to spend time with God. Conversely, each time the music began, a small entourage of women collected around the man on the floor below the stage's edge where he danced, separate from the many who flocked to the area all across the base of the stage, presumably to worship.

During the music, laser lights darted across the darkened room and a permeating, synthetic fog slowly crept up the aisles, working its way toward the back of the auditorium. (I quickly discovered that fog machines and respiratory distress—especially when combined with icy-cold air—can be an extremely uncomfortable combination. I spent much of these services unable to sing because I was coughing the entire time. Instead, I would quietly sit at the back and spend that time in prayer. I meditated on the lyrics of what the crowd was singing, remaining somewhat disconnected from the activities occurring around me, both for previously explained intellectual reasons and for those pertaining to my illness. At times, people did things that Donna and I struggled to understand: Their actions seemed more distracting and attention-seeking than what may have been motivated by true worship. Essentially, we felt awkward.

However, because of the multiple confirmations we had received regarding the trip and before leaving our hometown, Donna and I continued to attend every service, waiting for God to reveal the underlying reason He had brought us there. On the second-to-last day of the conference, between services, I stepped outside the auditorium and lined up at a nearby coffee to buy some herbal tea to both warm my body and soothe my chest and throat. As I observed those around me waiting to place their orders, it quickly became apparent that most of the others there were women who, like myself, had walked over from the conference. Realizing I was being intensely stared at by the woman next to me, I smiled in an attempt to alleviate awkwardness. Rather than looking away, the lady quickly shifted her weight and made intense eye contact, studying me. After a moment, she spoke.

"What's your calling?" I was taken aback by the question itself. It seemed very personal, not to mention completely out of left field. Yet, she boldly brought up the very question I had been praying about. I was in one of those "in-between" chapters, the kind in which one life phase has ended and a person wonders what is next. (The truth is, many things I had poured myself into previously had come to a screeching halt, and I had been praying "God, now what?" for quite a while. So, despite the fact that some would've been very off-put by the woman's intrusive question, I was immediately listening.)

"I'm honestly not sure yet," I met her gaze evenly. "I'm waiting for insight from God right now."

Part 3: Stepping Off the Island

"Can I pray for you?"

I knew she meant right there, right then, right in the middle of the coffee line. And you know what? That was fine by me. As I've stated, I'm usually that reserved girl, quietly praying in the corner—almost never the one at the center of the visible activity in such matters. But, I'm also willing to hear His voice any time or anywhere He chooses to reveal Himself to me, regardless of who's watching. This whole interaction had the feel of something divine, and if God was getting ready to tell me something, I was all ears. Yet, the logical side of my inner seeker was also on guard; I didn't want anything that wasn't really from God. I immediately began to internally pray, "God, I want to hear your voice, but only *your* voice. Please set a shield about my mind. Block out every other distraction, every other agenda, every false directive. Only *your* voice."

Immediately, the woman turned to a friend who had been standing next to her but who had turned to face the opposite direction to visit with another conference-goer. The three of us quickly exchanged first names (I'm going to call the one who initiated this conversation "Becky"). Becky announced that God was priming me to receive my calling; she said that they needed to pray for me.

And they did. Right then and there in the coffee line.

I bowed my head quietly as Becky and her friend laid hands on me and prayed for me. As Becky petitioned aloud, I experienced several confirmations through her words. By now, you've probably gathered that I'm not an overly mystical person, but she could never have known to pray for the specific things she did, or to use the very precise verbiage that she used. The answer to the question of calling didn't come in that moment, but I knew the appointment was ordained.

After ending the petition with the word "amen," Becky looked at me purposefully and pointed her finger at my chest. "God is going to tell you something tonight. During the song service this evening, go down and worship near the stage."

At the risk of sounding unspiritual, I will admit that, inwardly, I groaned a little. First of all, that was the area where the synthetic fog was the thickest, and I was still recovering from the inescapable dose I'd had of it during that morning's music. And, I still struggled with that awkward feeling of being the one who never seems to be struck with the same spirit of dancing or shouting that many others down front had already demonstrated the entire week. But I also believed in the core of my being that Becky had been divinely appointed to cross my path that day. So I nodded. "Okay, I will. And thank you for praying for me."

I turned to go find Donna and tell her what had happened. She had likewise had a few interactions with people throughout the week that we both believed had been divinely arranged, but each had taken place throughout our natural course of actions. For example, at lunch on one of the days, Donna had been given a specific message that she was compelled to tell our waitress. She felt a little awkward and struggled for a few moments with self-doubt, but—as anyone who knows Donna is aware—she is bold! Before long, she dismissed all second guessing and delivered the message. And, as God so often provides, there was confirmation that this woman had needed to hear that precise dispatch on that specific day. But, these were occurrences that took place organically—while they might have required the boldness to pray in the middle of a coffee line, or say something to a waitress, they were all occasions wherein we could respond to the circumstances that found their way to *us*. None required that we physically go anywhere other than we would have on our own.

This was different. Tonight, I would go down and stand amidst the showy laser lights, the dancers, the tambourine players, the flag-waving worshipers, and try to sing amidst the breath-aggravating fog. I would stand in a place where I felt completely *out of place*—and I would do it out of obedience.

The moment came for evening service to begin, and the music began to play. As if it had been awaiting its cue, fog began to work its way outward from the stage, climbing slowly up the sloped walkway and into the audience's part of the auditorium. I left my seat beside Donna and walked down to the crowded area around the stage, taking care to stand in an area far distanced from the male kinetic worshiper and his entourage. As I stood there, unable to sing due to my illness, I clasped my hands together, "praying-hands style," and raised my fingers to my chin. I bowed my head and closed my eyes. As I had done in earlier services, I meditated on the lyrics to the songs and maintained a prayerful state of mind. I alternated between worship of God and repeating the prayer that He would shield my mind from receiving any message except what He had for me. At one point, I felt a smack on my left shoulder and upper arm. I opened my eyes and noticed that somebody dancing had come too close to me and had accidentally slapped me. Her eyes looked at me as if to say "oops"; she grinned and kept dancing. I returned the smile and went back to my silent reverie. Minutes later, something similar happened on my right side, but the impact was to my leg this time. An individual who had fallen to the floor, seemingly slain in the spirit, had bumped me on her way down. She, however, made no eye contact, unaware that it had happened. I stepped aside several inches to give her room. Similar incidents continued to happen for the duration of the music. I began to wonder if, at some point, God was going to suddenly "hit me" with the undeniable and uncontrollable compulsion to dance or laugh, or if I, too, would possibly fall down, but none of these things happened. I was more than willing if that had been how His presence manifested to me, but I also did not want to get ahead of Him in such activity. Eventually, it became apparent that soon the song service would end. I felt certain that God had brought me to that place, at that specific moment, but I still didn't know *why*. Time was running out, and whatever reason God had for directing me there remained a mystery.

So my prayer changed.

"God, I only want to hear your voice. And if the lady today was wrong about you telling me something tonight, that's fine. I would rather hear from you at a much later time and know that it was *really* you speaking to me than to get some random word tonight that's not your voice. But God, I don't understand. I don't fit in. I don't worship like these people. I don't know how, and if I try without your prompting, I could end up faking it, which I believe is wrong. I want to worship you, but I want my worship to be real and not contrived. I don't understand why I'm different from these other people. I feel like I don't fit in. I'm just not like these people around me."

In that moment, the first nuggets of my answer came. And it was the beginning of God revealing to me the calling of my life, although the fullness of it came in layers of confirmation for several months after that. Before God would reveal my *calling* to me, He had to reveal my God-ordained *identity* to me.

"Exactly." I heard God say. Not audibly, but distinctly. "I don't want you to be like these other people. I don't even want you to try to be like these other people. I created you to be *you*. I want you to serve me like you and worship me like you. If it doesn't look the way other people think it should look, don't worry about it. I know your heart and your sincerity, and that's where true worship comes from."

That moment became a defining one in my life, one wherein I stopped feeling as if I were just a little bit more spiritual, my worship might look like someone else's. I let go of the nagging, internal suspicion that said if I were somehow a better Christian, maybe I would carry myself like others do when there is an exuberant and physical response at the altar. I realized that those who measured my spirituality by whether I followed all the same cues as other people in the room were judging by flawed criteria (this had happened often as a pastor's kid, and I'd even been called out for it publicly during altar calls in church).

Through this experience, God began to solidify in me His definition of who I am in Him, which provided the groundwork for the revelation of His calling on my life. Such an understanding brings so many things into perspective. When we comprehend what He sees when He looks at us, we realize that our accountability is to Him alone. Our service is for Him alone. Our purpose, identity, goals, strengths, abilities, talents, assets, attributes—even vulnerabilities and weaknesses—are all elements shaping and impacting the journey that should be to pursue Him alone and above all other things. Each of these factors that impact us daily can distract us and whittle away at our resources and energy, or they can each become refining elements that redirect us to move toward and lean on our Maker every day of our lives, in both big things and small.

Recently, I was attending another conference when I recalled my defining moment vividly. I sat amidst a group of people who were "gettin' rowdy for God!" The fired-up preacher was pacing quickly across the stage, and the responsive audience was shouting, waving their hands, and even standing and dancing during his sermon. Every now and then, he'd holler something like, "stand up and testify!"—at which approximately sixteen people sitting around me would immediately spring up, as though they had been ejected from a toaster, with their arms in the air, hands oscillating at the wrist. I, however, remained seated, clapped, and even made eye contact with the preacher while nodding. I don't know if I appeared out of place to anyone else, but I sat secure in the knowledge that I was not out of place in God's eyes. While in a different life chapter, I may have felt that I was lacking because I was different, I now draw from the understanding of what God told me at that ladies' conference those years ago.

God created an entire population of people who are misfits—each completely unique—and these eccentricities can and should be used to serve and worship Him in a variety of ways. More important than any kind of sameness in either of these avenues of interaction with Him is that it is from the heart, sincere, and dedicated to Him first and foremost.

On a Practical Note

I mentioned attending churches where those who didn't seem to be showing enough physical exuberance during worship risked being called out publicly. Services at one church often featured altar calls wherein each pew was almost completely empty because all attendees were gathered at the front of the sanctuary. This is a beautiful thing if God is moving in mighty ways and all altar-goers are there voluntarily, but often that wasn't the case. The pastor (not my own dad, who never did this) would point at the few folks still lingering in their seats, saying things like, "You there in the back, it's time to let go of what you're holding on to. Come up here and give it to God, right now!" (Nobody was safe from such pinpointing. Once a friend who had been upstairs working in children's church—thus had missed most of the sermon—had come down to stand in the back of the auditorium for the last moments of the service. Despite his extremely late arrival, the preacher said to him, "You, sir—I've been watching you through this entire service. You need to come up here so we can pray for you.") Such awkward moments resulted in a no-win situation for the person still seated, who was now the focus of the entire assembly. If those being called out didn't have a particular prayer request at that moment, they faced either having to walk down the church aisle in front of everyone, possibly requesting intercession for any random thing that came to mind as a result of being put on the spot or choosing to sit still despite the minister's request, and then appearing unspiritual or obstinate. Most members often chose the path of least resistance by preemptively going to the altar at the end of every service to avoid such a dilemma—hence the rows of empty seats.

However, a pattern I noticed among many churches I observed over the years was that many that carried out this practice also had significant issues of spiritual invasion or even demonic infiltration. (Much more about this can be read in *Everyday Champions* by Joe Horn.) The leadership of one particular congregation actually reported the presence of demons crawling up and down the walls of their sanctuary during services, and made inquiries with my dad, the pastor at the time, regarding how to deal with this issue.[52] Some who "danced in the spirit" actually engaged in salacious physical interaction with people who were not their spouses after meeting at the altar to each pray separately over marital troubles. Other manifestations that should have been brought into check occurred, but many were unaware of the circumstances since the focus of the service had been taken off of worshiping and serving God and placed on either individuals' emotional experiences or their attempts to navigate the experience without being called out.

This is devastating to a congregation, because when we allow God to define our identity before Him, He directs as our diverse approaches to service and worship strengthen and support each other while simultaneously keeping one another in check.

When we're allowed to spiritually thrive in the way that God has aligned our heart, soul, and mind to flow, free of the worry that others will measure their responses and pass judgment regarding our spirituality, we are at liberty to interact with God aside from a manmade checklist of criteria. Also, perhaps those who are allowed without censure to remain seated or standing at the back of the church during worship services or altar calls can objectively observe what's going on. Then, if some of the activities start to go awry (such as the inappropriate dancing), they're in a position to notice it and intervene.

Consider secular activities such as a rock concert or sports event. Many in the crowds become emotional and excited, often cheering, clapping, jumping up out of their seats, and dancing. There's usually nothing wrong with this response. Yet, at each of these events, security officers are always stationed throughout the crowd. We would never see a member of the security team dancing at the stage during a concert (well, let's just say a security team member wouldn't do it *twice*). Those personnel are stationed to watch the crowd for potential problems. Why should the (often highly emotional) church services be any different?

Finding Your Unique Place in the Body

Much of the focus of this section has been on altar manifestations because that topic is essential in the narrative of my own story of spiritual identity. But the point I'm making goes much further than worship responses. When people measure the impact of their interactions with God via the measuring stick of physical manifestations, comparison with other Christians, or other parameters that are set by mankind instead of God, our focus is drawn to those matters instead of to Him. The fruit of His presence in our lives is not recognized for what it is, which cheapens our appreciation of His operations within us. Furthermore, those who want to connect with the Body of Christ but find themselves unable to associate with the mainstream crowd might leave Christianity because their basis for comparison isn't accurate in the first place.

The key to beginning to grow spiritually—as an individual, as a Church, and in ministry—is by realizing and embracing the fact that we're not all cut from the same cloth. In fact, our greatest strengths are often found in our diversities and eccentricities. God did not invite us into His Kingdom to homogenize us into a congregation of cookie-cutter followers. He created a population of unique people who, when united under His purposes, can serve Him with a fuller and more thorough capacity than we ever can when we live under the scrutiny of trying to be like others. Once we embrace our inner oddball, we become free to find His identity for us and His calling on our lives, and we can even discover the fullness of our own unique way of serving Him. By allowing ourselves to find the misfit within, we become free to experience the distinctive abundance that He has for each of us; we begin to live our *own* story.

You have a special destiny in the Body of Christ, but you'll never find it by trying to be like anyone around you. If God made you with a one-of-a-kind set of skills, talents, and perspectives, then surely He wouldn't want to see it wasted in trade for a version of you that fits another person's mold!

By embracing your inner-misfit, you can courageously embark on a journey wherein you can discover your dynamic and thriving individuality and, ultimately, everything that our Creator destined you to be.

6

Letting Go of the Lie

By Donna Howell, Allie Henson, and Nita Horn

What Makes a Misfit, Anyway?

Ultimately, when studying the residents of the Island of Misfit Toys, the question that seems to cross everyone's mind is *why* they were doomed to live in exile. Are we to believe that a simple difference of appearance or function is such a profound nonconformity that these toys must live a life of banishment—as though a small deviation from the characteristics of their peers is weighty enough to condemn them to a life of seclusion?

We say the word "no" with our mouths, yet, our actions often tell another story as we withdraw from others because of our differences. Sadly, one of the places we see this division from others occur with the greatest devastation is when it takes place within the Body of Christ (more on this in the upcoming pages). So, *who* is it that we are hardest on when it's time to ostracize? For many of us, the answer to this question is *ourselves*.

One Is the... Safest Number

Though the inhabitants of the Island of Misfit Toys are, we can infer, there in exile because someone sent them there (even though the playthings seem very much to be still useful and loveable), many of us are in isolation because *we've placed ourselves there* (again, like the misfits, even though we are in fact very much still useful and worthy of love.) We do this because we are keenly aware of our own scars, shortcomings, failures, past traumas, insecurities, and vulnerabilities. Interacting with others beyond a certain point requires opening up and being transparent about such private issues. We all "manage" these issues in different ways. Some of us bravely put on a façade of normalcy, hoping that nobody sees behind the veil of success, wealth, or other "I've-got-my-act-together"-isms. Others retreat behind a flurry of drama of some sort, always seeking a circumstance or peer to blame for any perception of personal shortcomings. And still others of us—a small percentage, to be sure—are transparent, confessing where we lack strength and continually working to self-improve.

But many of us hide. At the appearance of what we perceive to be an unlovely aspect of ourselves, we put up a wall to retreat behind—alone. Many of us become so accustomed to this isolation that we pull off engaging in an entire lifetime of relationships at arm's length; we trade the safety of isolation for the intimacy of complicated, often messy, human relationships.

The irony in such cases is that, like with many of the toys, others are unable to see what our debilitating issue even is. In fact, we're not usually even looking for it! For example, many toys on the island, including the scooter, the soldiers, and the cars, appear to have no flaws at all. The viewers find themselves thinking, "Wait a minute, there's nothing wrong with that plaything. Why is *it* stuck out there with the misfits?" For others, the query becomes, "Okay, so that toy is a little different than other toys. But a child could *totally* still play with it. The flaw doesn't render it unusable. So, why the dramatic exile to an island of outcasts?

Yet, many of us do this to ourselves each day in all arenas: family, work, school, communities, and even church. In fact, I daresay that the church is one of the first places this happens. For many, attendance at any sort of religious institution carries a stigma that goes one of two directions: It's either a competition to see who can appear to be the most pious (with that piety usually being laced with hypocrisy) or a continual measuring-up of righteousness that falls short of allowing anyone the opportunity to make a real and lasting contribution. On one hand, people become disenchanted and want no part of the scene. On the other, they never feel they measure up, so they assume they have nothing to contribute.

Typecast Ministerial Roles

Another reason people isolate from the Body of Christ is the formulaic typecasting of ministerial roles that seems to take place often in the church. For example, say someone recently converted to Christianity and wants to be used by God. Most people have a chapter like this in their own lives after they begin to experience Christ's transformative power. Thus, it's not unusual at all for such spiritual newcomers to approach church leadership with an interest in serving.

Unfortunately, this offer of ministerial help is all too often met with a narrative that goes something like this:

"It's great that you want to serve! Here's what we have open right now… The adult Sunday school class needs a teacher, we need help with the two-and-three-year-old vacation Bible school class, there are church building repair/work days on Saturdays, and we always need more janitors."

Understanding first that service to the Lord comes in many forms, each of these roles, of course, is vastly important. If you've been serving in any of these areas, kudos to you! We're simply mentioning these to lead into a recent convert's typical reaction, which might go something like this:

"I don't yet know enough about the Bible to feel like I could teach it to adults. I work weeknights/am intimidated by babies, so the toddler class isn't a good fit for me. I have some valid reason (perhaps a work schedule, family events, or health condition) that keeps me from being able to give my Saturdays to building maintenance and repair. Does this mean that the only way to serve/grow closer to God is by being a janitor?"

(Before continuing, please allow us to say that Allie was a janitor for several years, and we're in no way disparaging the occupation. In fact, Allie enjoyed it for many reasons! It was hard enough work that she stayed physically fit. It was solitary work, so she was left alone all day long—just God, her, and her music-loaded earbuds. And, as long as everything was clean when she left, there was no interpersonal drama, no coworker politics, and no boss breathing down her neck. It was great! So please, understand, the mention of such a vital job is not to pick on it. In fact, first impressions of a church occur *because* of self-sacrificing individuals who make sure that the facilities are pristine. This boosts a newcomer's confidence in the organization as a whole, making them feel safer about bringing their children in and even elevating the credibility of such unseen elements as doctrine. After all, those who are meticulous about their work will give the impression of having done due diligence in other areas as well.)

The issue as it pertains to recent converts asking to be involved in ministry is the fact that they're often struggling to put a more complex question into words when they approach church leadership about serving. As they begin to experience God's transformational power in their lives, they're looking for a deeper interaction with Him, His people, His Body, and His work. In any believers who see the fruit of God's work in their lives, a connection to the Great Commission should begin to fuel their drive toward action. Often, the unspoken goal they envision is to reach people for Christ, improve the world around them, and find their own, unique calling therein. Having no idea how to put this into words to form a request, they often approach church leadership with a generic interest "to serve." (Additionally, the request is usually so outside of their comfort zone that they're afraid they'll be told "no," which would exacerbate their vulnerability.) In any case, to summarize, new believers are often unsure of how to close the gap between what they believe serving in a thriving ministry looks like and the cold, hard truth about less dynamic avenues of service.

For many, the "disconnect" we've just described causes some people to withdraw from religion altogether, believing that it worked for a while but that they somehow lost the life-changing momentum they had at first. Others may separate themselves from the Body, deciding that Christianity is something better pursued on their own, often without being involved in a local church. While some who take this road continue to stay in the Word and grow closer to God, others find it leads to an open-ended search for a more generic "truth"; a syncretistic, blended religion with Jesus somewhere still at the center becomes the focus while a singular, biblical truth is lost along the way. Another group remains in the Church, but each person in it self-isolates because they don't understand what it means to be a part of the Body of Christ.

In a nutshell, we within the Body of Christ have forgotten who we are and who He created us to be. We've replaced the dynamic and evangelistic vision of individuals all serving God with passion and sincerity with tired, typecast, automated obedience. In so doing, we fall into a mindset of survival: Much of our fervent desire to connect with others shuts down, and we further withdraw. It becomes an unending cycle. (While the issue of modern church relevance is outside the scope of this book, this is a huge contributing factor to why the Church has become so disconnected from its surrounding society.)

Additionally, when discussing reasons modern churchgoers self-isolate, we find that many of these issues are present in congregants' personal lives even before they arrive at church.

What does all this have to do with the misfit toys? We'll certainly come back to that throughout this chapter, but before getting into the specifics, let's just say that most of the toys' shortcomings are in their own minds. And that brings us to the crux of many of our problems. You see, just as many of the residents of the Island of Misfit Toys may have been able to move on to live fulfilling lives *not* exiled, their own belief that they must be isolated under the label of "misfit" kept them doing precisely that. And the truth is, we're not so different. If we can each heal and redirect our own mind, we can, once and for all, shed the label that banishes us.

7

Renew Your Mind

By Donna Howell, Allie Henson, and Nita Horn

As we've seen, the conversation surrounding what's keeping the toys in exile on the Island of Misfit Toys is largely their own inability to overlook the ways they're different from their peers. This kind of battle—*the one that occurs within our own thoughts*—is a good starting point for addressing how to redeem misfits—whether it's the toys or our own selves—back into society. As we tackle this issue, we'll discuss these thought processes and their implications in the Body of Christ as well. There is much to be said for the renewing of our minds: It is both Scriptural and practical.

We find the following scriptural command regarding such renewal in Romans 12:2:

> And be not conformed to this world: but be ye transformed by the renewing of your mind, that ye may prove what is that good, and acceptable, and perfect, will of God.

In 2 Corinthians 10:3–5, which we'll refer to in-depth in the coming pages, further elaborates:

For though we walk in the flesh, we do not war after the flesh: (For the weapons of our warfare are not carnal, but mighty through God to the pulling down of strong holds;) Casting down imaginations, and every high thing that exalteth itself against the knowledge of God, and bringing into captivity every thought to the obedience of Christ.

This passage is profound and yet often underappreciated. In essence, it states that we live in the realm of the flesh, but that's not where our battle occurs. In fact, the methods of our warfare are mighty enough to remove strongholds—this means break bondage!—through the power of God. This is accompanied by surrendering our own ungodly or false narratives and filtering *every* thought until the only ones we allow to remain in our minds are those that follow God's will.

Sounds pretty, right? It is, but it's also much easier said than done. And, the right kind of covert attack from the enemy can cause us to misinterpret which thoughts to stop and which ones to feed.

It's important to grasp this distinction moving forward. Many people can easily identify the enemy's tactics of destruction, which might include the temptation of wrongdoing, such as falling into addictions, engaging in crimes, committing marital infidelity, and demonstrating the traits of greed and pride. These kinds of pitfalls, while less obvious to those who land in them, are usually easy to spot for those whose weaknesses lie in other areas.

On the other hand, some people, those whose downfall may simply be self-defeat, don't so easily identify the evil one's method, because it's often a lie that feels as though it comes from within. For example, some attacks don't appear dressed as salacious temptations that can lure us off the path of the righteous in an attempt to render us ineffective in the Body of Christ. Instead, these assaults bar our ability to grow spiritually by presenting such covert lies as, "I could live a more potent spiritual life and even reach others for the Kingdom, if only I were smart enough," or, "If I were pretty enough, rich enough, organized, charismatic, extroverted, etc., enough…" Because those of us who engage in these thought patterns will never measure up to our own self-critiquing, the enemy has us right where he wants us—and strategy is so subtle that we do nothing to fight back, never realizing it for what it is—an attack.

The lies we believe, then, become a self-administered poison that isolates us under the belief that our damage, shortcomings, or vulnerabilities render our banishment to be in everyone's best interests (as well as what's best for our own emotional and psychological safety), and we withdraw. Often, along with each progressive state of exile comes an even deeper sense of failure and loneliness, perpetuating the situation.

Recording artist Francesca Batistelli sings a song called "If We're Honest," in which she tackles this issue. The lyrics beautifully explain how we can reverse this fragmentation within the Body of Christ:

Truth is harder than a lie.
The dark seems safer than the light.
And everyone has a heart that loves to hide.
I'm a mess and so are you.
We've built walls nobody can get through.
Yeah, it may be hard, but the best thing we could ever do
Is bring your brokenness, and I'll bring mine.
'Cause love can heal what hurt divides.
And mercy's waiting on the other side, if we're honest.[53]

If we're *honest*. Huh. What a thought. Wonder what such a notion could look like?

Perhaps it could look like this: Transparent, vulnerable, damaged people gathering under the heading of making the world a better place and reaching people for the Savior. Such a collective would be willing to face their shortcomings while harnessing their strengths. They would use their available resources and maximize their natural abilities with the understanding that a community built on Christ is filled with flawed, but ever-improving, forgiven people who want to reach others and share God's love.

Kind of sounds like an evangelistic, dynamic, relevant, community-reaching body of believers, doesn't it?

The concept is rudimentary and simplistic, but is somehow difficult for many to grasp. Of course, everybody wants to be transparent and vulnerable, to be willing to coexist with others in a form of community where everyone's strengths *and* weaknesses are understood, embraced, and encouraged. Yet, there is something inside each of us that seems to say that everyone around us has permission to be flawed or have baggage, but that we personally have no such luxury. Each of us is so much harder on ourselves than we are on those around us, and the result is that we build walls to hide the real "us" behind veils of perfection, success, beauty, charisma, joy, talent, and/or other attributes that seem more "presentable" than the damaged individual who resides inside our skin. Many of us innately understand that it's this hiding that keeps us from fulfilling the beautiful calling that God has placed on each of our lives. How do we open up and get beyond this self-abasement that keeps us from ever reaching our potential? And, what do we do with the fear of opening up and then being hurt by others to whom we've exposed our true, inner selves?

How Do We Open Up?

The answers to this question often come in clumsy form: "You gotta start somewhere," or "Just jump in!" People utter phrases such as these in an effort to muster the strength to become vulnerable when analytical answers don't avail themselves. And these responses do hold some truth. After all, nobody can calculate all the risks of interpersonal interaction, then present a foolproof plan for navigating such dynamics. (If so, the person who figured this out would be a wealthy individual, indeed!)

However, there are a few things to remember when tackling such questions, each of which will be elaborated upon in the upcoming pages: 1) It helps to give ourselves as much grace as we give others; 2) not everybody's pitfall is an obvious "temptation" (as mentioned earlier); and 3) it is through scripturally tackling the pitfalls of the mind that we can be unleashed from bondage.

Giving Ourselves Grace

First, it's important to remember that some people are so hard on themselves that they leave no room for anyone else to even correct them. For example, we authors know a woman who is a devout and loving person who seeks God with all her heart. Usually, any offenses she happens to commit are accidental—a hastily spoken word or an unintentionally inconsiderate act. By the time she realizes she's done something wrong or hurtful, she's so quick to mentally beat herself up there is no room for anyone else to do anything but enter the scene with grace and mercy. However, this young woman is so loving and gracious to those around her that, often, those who have made mistakes similar to hers are immediately forgiven without even needing an apology. Balanced with her tender approach are the carefully but firmly stated stances of biblical doctrine in all she does. This makes her a loving and sound advisor for her peers.

Several times, this woman has beaten herself up over mistakes of her past, or she has overanalyzed her own actions in ways that she would never do to another. It seems that while she is the first to extend forgiveness to others, she struggles to forgive herself. Yet, once God has forgiven us, we must forgive ourselves in order to move forward. There is a simple trick that helps in such cases.

The idea is for us to "step outside of ourselves" for just a moment, and talk to ourselves as though the side of us needing reprimand or advice is someone else. For those of us who tend to be harder on ourselves than we should be, this helps us to give the same grace to ourselves that we quickly show to other people. Ironically, the people who are hardest on themselves are usually the most gracious to those around them. If you are someone who struggles with self-forgiveness, shouldn't you give yourself the same grace that you would give another person? Some people even talk out loud to themselves, saying the kind words they would speak to another person. The method you use doesn't matter, as long as it frees your mind from the mistakes of the past.

The bottom line is, for some people, the pitfall of the enemy's attack isn't found in typically recognized forms of temptation, but instead is found in the self-abasement that we are willing to put ourselves through.

It's Not Always Obvious

Second, it's good to keep in mind that many "temptations" are found in what most people within the church would quickly identify as being from a sinful origin. For some, addiction of all types (substance abuse, pornography, gambling, etc.) may be a weakness. For others, pride may be a downfall that causes spiritual slip-ups. For still others, pursuits of worldly matters such as greed, money, fame, popularity, and acclaim may hinder their spiritual growth.

But then, there are other people...

These are the ones whose attack happens within the mind. Because this is such a subtle and covert tactic, it is difficult to recognize. In these cases, people don't necessarily need to commit a sinful act in order for this tactic to hinder their spiritual growth. Since there is no catalyst action or intentional will behind this method of attack, it often appears to stem from internal sources that veil its ability to manifest as spiritual combat or lie from the enemy. Problems with self-esteem, lack of confidence, the feeling that one is damaged—virtually any type of inward pain that keeps someone from reaching out to other people—become the bonds by which Satan limits a person's connection to the body of

Christ *and* one's usefulness within it. This isn't always recognized for the spiritual warfare that it is for two reasons: 1) As has been stated, its source is not found in overt wrongdoing that comes about as a result of temptation; and 2) life is hard and circumstances have a way of scarring people and making them develop their own fears that are also human in origin. It would be untrue to say that humanity is, in and of itself, incapable of thinking fearful or vulnerable thoughts. However, people forget that Satan has been studying mankind—*deceiving* mankind—since the Garden of Eden. If such issues have even a seedling in someone's mind, they can be exploited by the one who wants to see that person's downfall. Those who follow God with all of their heart, or even who have a moral compass that steers them away from obvious sin, may not fall into the traps. These individuals are *watching* for that type of deception. On the other hand, these are often people who seek to be humble, pious, and unselfish—all of which are good traits. But when this desire for goodness is coupled with a willingness to be hard on oneself, this well-meaning trait can be exploited and twisted into the lie that we must try to daily earn our status with God instead of receiving it as the gift of grace that it is. When this happens, we lose the context of what God has created us to be, and forget the mercy He has given to each of us because of His great love for us. We become so preoccupied with what we are not, and so isolated from the Body of Christ, that we can become stagnant in our walk with God or in our ability to serve Him. This is because we are so certain of our unworthiness that we disregard the great gift of worth that He has placed on our lives through His redemption.

And in it all, we lose track of the potential that we have in operating within the Kingdom of God, because we daily remind ourselves that we have no worthy place in it. Potential ministries never begin, lives that could be touched remain unaffected, and our senses of failure and isolation deepen. It's the most covert attack on the Body of Christ, and it's an erosion from the inside out. It's completely unnecessary, if we could simply realize that *we* are the toys that actually have differences, but not defects. We're so good at seeing our own damage. *If only* we could see ourselves through His eyes.

The Mind Is Freed by Believing Scripture

The third thing to remember when trying to figure out how to open up to others and become involved in the Body of Christ (or other groups of family and peers, for that matter), is to remember that the bondage of the mind is freed by embracing and *believing* Scripture. This may seem oversimplified, but remember that while we said the Bible provides the key, we never said it was easy. Battles that occur within the mind can be some of the most debilitating, because they stem from the base of our psyche that involves our experiences, our fears, our memories, our vulnerabilities, and even philosophical arenas such as our moral compass and religious and spiritual convictions. And, as mentioned, these skirmishes can be difficult to recognize because they don't always derive from a cognitive choice or intentional action, but from a place embedded more deeply within us.

For many, shaking the negative, self-abusing thoughts that keep us limited is the first—and often the biggest—step. So, for the reader who has struggled on this note, we will begin to lay a scriptural foundation from which we hope you can derive your future self-image.

We will begin with Psalm 139:12–16:

[God,] even the darkness is not dark to you; the night is bright as the day, for darkness is as light with you. For you formed my inward parts; you knitted me together in my mother's womb. I praise you, for I am fearfully and wonderfully made. Wonderful are your works; my soul knows it very well. My frame was not hidden from you, when I was being made in secret, intricately woven in the depths of the earth. Your eyes saw my unformed substance; in your book were written, every one of them, the days that were formed for me, when as yet there was none of them." (ESV)

This passage reveals a handful of truths that people should understand about their standing with God. First of all, nothing is hidden from Him. All the secret vulnerabilities and insecurities that we try to hide from our peers are completely exposed to God. When God's Word tells us that He loves us, He does—even with full knowledge of our shortcomings.

Additionally, this passage is very clear that our design, from the earliest moment, was created with God's supervision and awareness. The most intricate, obscure elements of our being are ones that God is not only aware of, but that He Himself knit together. He wrote each of our stories in His book, and He has orchestrated our days.

Do you understand what this Scripture is really saying? *Nothing* about you is an accident, a surprise—an "oops"—that God just later made work.

Nothing. Every little flaw, fear, finitely human tendency that you have is one God allowed to remain. He watched each fiber of your being as it was formed in the deepest, most secret places of the universe. He could have made you differently than you are. He was there. He watched it. He had the time and the wherewithal to intervene. So why didn't He do things differently?

In the film *Anne of Green Gables* based on the novel by Lucy Maud Montgomery, Anne, a stubborn and imaginative orphan, sees the source of many of her life's troubles as having sprung from the fact that her hair is red. When Marilla, Anne's would-be adoptive mother, asks if the girl has said her nightly prayers. Anne replies, "Mrs. Hammond [a former authority figure] told me that God made my hair red on purpose, and I've never cared for Him since."[54] Marilla then firmly informs Anne that while she lives under her roof, she *will* do so, and then teaches the young girl how. (Despite the rebellious nature of the Anne's comment, this film reinforces faith, promotes a wholesome moral compass, and generally depicts a simpler time of innocence. In fact, these authors highly recommend this movie—particularly the 1985 version directed by Kevin Sullivan—for families with children of all ages.)

While many might accuse such a statement of indicating obstinance toward the Maker, if we're honest, we've each felt similar feelings over the course of our lives. If the Creator of all watched and even directed as we were molded, then *why* wouldn't He have intervened and removed our flaws as we were forming?

Let's back up to the very beginning, when God was examining what He created:

And God saw every thing that he had made, and, behold, it was very *good.* (Genesis 1:31; emphasis added)

In this passage, the word "good" derives from the Hebrew *tôwb* or *tobe,* meaning "pleasant" or "agreeable."[55] God saw that what He had created—including the man and woman He had fashioned—and, knowing in advance all other human beings who would walk the earth, and found them to be not *perfect*—not *without flaw,* but agreeable and pleasant in His sight. This was, of course, before sin entered the scene, which introduced a new level of susceptibility to evil in our nature, but even at this point, we were agents of free will and capable of being misled. We know this to be true, because Adam and Eve soon disobeyed God (Genesis 3).

We see in this passage that God saw the good in us and found us to be pleasant. So, why wouldn't He make us completely perfect, above any kind of moral dilemma or fear, impermeable to vulnerability or insecurity? It seems that a race of flawless superhumans would tell such a more effective testimony of our Mighty God, would we not?

Mankind's choice to turn away from God at the first recorded opportunity shows that this notion makes for a nice theory, but it's not a likely reality. Humanity's hearts are given to evil thoughts, lusts, violence, disloyalty, deception, and pride, while the flesh lives at constant odds with the will of God (Mark 7:21; Jeremiah 17:9; Jeremiah 17:23; Galatians 5:17). In other words, left to our own devices, we quickly forget our Maker and follow our own selfish desires. We need a constant reminder of who made us, a constant lifeline that connects us to Him. The Apostle Paul understood this all too well:

> So to keep me from becoming conceited because of the surpassing greatness of the revelations, a thorn was given me in the flesh, a messenger of Satan to harass me, to keep me from becoming conceited. Three times I pleaded with the Lord about this, that it should leave me. But he said to me, "My grace is sufficient for you, for my power is made perfect in weakness." Therefore I will boast all the more gladly of my weaknesses, so that the power of Christ may rest upon me. For the sake of Christ, then, I am content with weaknesses, insults, hardships, persecutions, and calamities. For when I am weak, then I am strong. (2 Corinthians 12:7–10; ESV)

We see this sentiment echoed in Psalms 50:15:

> And call upon me in the day of trouble: I will deliver thee, and thou shalt glorify me.

The implication here seems self-explanatory, and can be generalized to all of humanity: God allows us to face weakness of all types because it reminds us who carries us. In our time of trouble, He assists us or delivers us; we, in turn, glorify Him for doing that.

Isn't this ironic? We hide because we're so keenly aware of our imperfections, yet those very flaws are our ticket to a closer walk with God—and a connection to those who truly are His people. The very shortcoming that may have made you—the reader—withdraw from Christ and His Church should be the very thing drawing you to connectivity! Every flaw, temptation, scar, insecurity, and fear is an opportunity to reach out to a Loving Savior who holds the answer. These inadequacies offer us a chance to beckon to our Heavenly Father, who formed our hearts in the deepest and most mysterious places of the universe, and who now holds them in His hand when our earthly fathers have either failed us or exhausted all solutions. They leave an unresolved and nagging pain inside us that can only be mended by the Holy Spirit's ministry of peace that surpasses the understanding of all humanity (Philippians 4:7).

And, here's the best part:

Being confident of this very thing, that he which hath begun a good work in you will perform it until the day of Jesus Christ. (Philippians 1:6)

How does it feel to be the pet project of the Most High God? The Maker of everything not only took the time, way back when, to *start* a good work in you, but He's willing to keep at it until Jesus returns! This doesn't mean until He gets bored, until you mess up again, until someone prettier or someone with more potential comes along; it means until the end of this age. For the rest of your life on earth. The only thing that will stop His work in your life is for you to decide you don't want His help or input.

Should you be embarrassed about your shortcomings? No, they're the lifeline that keeps you connected to the Maker who wants to build you up daily and make you a better person. Should you hide because of them? No! If they remind you daily of your need for the Lord, and the pursuit of healing continually draws you closer to Him as His child, then realize that every other true follower of Christ is experiencing his or her own version of the same journey. And the lack of this realization is a lie that has divided the Church from the inside out.

Part 3: Stepping Off the Island

Now What About That Narrative?

When we doubt our ability to serve God or His Body, we are downplaying the goodness, talent, abilities, creativity, and other attributes that God gave us. When we sell ourselves short, we think that we are only insulting ourselves. However, when this negative narrative impedes our connection to God or fellow believers, we elevate our flawed, self-abasing thought pattern above the knowledge of God, which states His love and happiness with us and His confidence in our potential. This is a strange, backward pride we sometimes illustrate by prioritizing our self-abusive thoughts over the positive chronicle that God Himself has spoken over our lives. This brings us back to a previously made point, which is that we can reverse this thinking by embracing Scripture's statement that we are an up-and-coming work in progress; we're destined to be overcomers and more than conquerors (Romans 8:37).

The first step is to see in ourselves the value that God sees—to understand that our very origin was found first in Him; at the end, He will hold each of us and wipe the tears from our eyes, telling us that we now belong to a world that knows no pain or sorrow (Revelation 21). This is our final destination as God's people!

So, do you still think you're not smart, funny, organized, pretty, talented, creative, charismatic, or [insert your own shortcoming here] enough to be involved in God's kingdom? Or perhaps your hobbies or interests are so obscure that you can't imagine a way they might be used at church. Every storyline that plays itself out in your mind to keep you from reaching the full potential that you have in God's Kingdom is a spiritual lie that limits your growth and your Kingdom contribution. Even more covert and malevolent is the fact that these self-restrictive thought patterns, when we don't bring them into check as 2 Corinthians 10:3–5 instructs, exalt themselves against the knowledge of God. They hinder our progress and our ability to truly connect and exchange with other believers, and impede our ability to reach others for the Kingdom in our own unique way. When the self-abuse has become the script we believe instead of what God has clearly told us about our potential, we subscribe to a backward, sneaky type of pride: We become so down on ourselves and so consumed with the self-punishment that we raise up that understanding *over* the one given to us by our Creator, which says that we are loved, we are beautifully and wonderfully made, we have value, we have gifts, we have individually unique forms of service, and that each of us is so innately valuable to the Kingdom of God that He mourns over each of us who is lost (Matthew 18:10—14) and all of heaven celebrates as each of us is gained (Luke 15:7).

Dear reader, if you are believing the lie that you have nothing to give, that you cannot serve, or that you're not unique or "good enough" to blend with the rest of the believers, you're falling for a sinister lie. And, it is time to trade that story in, exchanging it for the knowledge of a God who thinks the world of you.

8

Are You Inspired? That's Too Bad...

By Donna Howell, Allie Henson, and Nita Horn

As mentioned earlier, Allie struggled for years with such words as "inspired" or "enthusiastic" because she found them to be emotional terms people would subscribe to the flavor of the month—whatever it may be. But, as the emotion wore off, so did the momentum. It bothered her to watch, because it seemed as though many folks didn't have any control over their actions, but instead were commanded by the uncontrollable "feeling" that seemed to carry them to and fro, "like leaves in the wind at the mercy of whither we blow."[56] Essentially, she found that such words usually meant that people were "on a kick" that would lack any real staying-power in their life.

So, imagine her reaction to being asked to help write this "inspirational" book. The last thing we would ever want to do is foster someone's short-lived, robust response to any given direction or cause that is not well thought out, possibly not God-ordained, and thus will not last. Vital energetic resources are wasted in such cases, and that would break our hearts. So, at this point, we'll ask you, the reader, "Are you inspired? Do you feel enthusiastic? Excited? Impassioned?"

If the answer is an exuberant "yes," bolstered with a bouncing need to expel this morning's extra breakfast calories, then we daresay we're disappointed. Why? Because once your latte has worn off, there's the chance that it will take with it the drive that currently fuels your purpose.

Unless you understand what you're *truly* saying when you call yourself these things.

"I'm Inspired"

Let's begin by discussing the word "inspire." During the years when Allie cringed at the word, she had yet to understand what it *really* meant, and that was a big game-changer.

> All Scripture is given by inspiration of God, and is profitable for doctrine, for reproof, for correction, for instruction in righteousness, that the man of God may be perfect, thoroughly furnished unto all good works. (2 Timothy 3:16–17)

Wait a minute—does this passage mean that God got really excited, and giddy, and in His thrilled jitters He threw out something that we use for dogmatic boundaries, rectification, and religious teaching? As silly as it may seem, that's what Allie and many others may have thought about this passage. But that assessment doesn't balance…

Unless "inspire" means something else. Turns out, it does.

Upon doing a brief etymological study, we find that though the word "inspire" *does* have an emotional connotation at times, but is not limited to emotions. The mechanics of the word break down as follows: It is built upon the Latin prefix *in*, meaning to put "in or into, on or upon,"[57] and the *spiritus*. The latter term at times denotes the concept of the sound of moving air, such as breathing, wind, whistling, or "blowing into," which directly connects the term to the notion of one's soul.[58]

According to the *Oxford Dictionary of English Etymology*, however, the word "inspire," when put together, actually takes on a uniquely spiritual element—it's not just emotional state. It defines the word as to "infuse into the mind; impart or suggest by a divine agency."[59]

So, when we say that Scripture is inspired by God, and we understand the true meaning of the word, we realize that God breathed His own Word into authors who wrote according to His instructions through the means provided by His power and authority. It is *His* essence, exhaled from Himself and put into human beings who become sanctioned to fulfill His directive. It's strangely similar to when, in Genesis 2:7, God "breathed" (Hebrew *nâphach*, meaning literally to blow[60]) life into man's nostrils at the point of his creation.

This was God's original inspiration into mankind. He filled us with life through the power of His breath. He gave us purpose when He filled our lungs with air. And He empowered those who wrote His Word, carried out His work, and spread His Great Commission with His divine impartation. *He* alone holds the power to inspire us, to call us, to empower us.

Inspiration is *not* feeling giddy about a new path, relationship, or project. It is not drawn from going to a religious camp or conference and listening to a speaker who ramps up the crowd for a week or two. It's not too much coffee alongside a sugary muffin and a cool, new idea that sounds fun.

And, it *should never* wear off...

Inspiration is the consistent, life-long empowerment to follow what God reveals—including our calling and identity in Him—*for as long as there is breath in our lungs.*

So, we ask you again: Are you feeling inspired? (Now if you say "yes," we will be so happy!)

Many words and their true meanings have unjustly been sold short in today's vocabulary, so we miss their depth of meaning. If only we knew what power these words could hold with a proper understanding of their definition and usage. There are many examples; we'll quickly visit a few.

"I Feel Passionate"

While the word "passion" often refers to romantic love or arousal, to be "impassioned" actually means something much deeper. It is defined by components of suffering and pain, infused with a "powerful affection of the mind," which, at its origin, referred to the suffering of Jesus on the Cross.[61] (Because of the connection between angst and love, this word has morphed to describe an emotional, combative outburst.) The roots of the word in fact outline the intensity of the self-sacrificing adoration Christ suffered greatly for on behalf of those for whom He laid down His life. When we say we follow God with "passion," the word doesn't mean that our emotions will always be positive and that we'll enjoy the whole experience. It means that, come what may, we remain faithful to Him as Job did: "Though he slay me, yet will I trust in him... He also shall be my salvation" (Job 13:15, 16).

"I Feel Enthusiastic"

"Enthusiasm," derived from the Greek components *en* and *theos*, literally means "god-possessed."[62] It stands for something more than a cheerleader who shouts loudly and makes crisp moves with a bright smile; it means to be completely owned by God and frenzied, zealous, and inspired[63] toward a God-owned cause. Those who think they've been called to serve a purpose must understand that to truly be enthusiastic about it means that they'll acknowledge that *their entire life* belongs to God, even when that includes unpleasant circumstances. One young woman recently met a man who seemed perfect for her until God revealed to her that he wasn't the one. The woman had to make the hurtful decision to let him go. This was an act of faith showing that she believed God would send another, better match at the right time. In a conversation with her friend, the comrade pointed out the young man's good qualities (which were many!) and urged the woman to reconsider. The answer was both impassioned with the woman's love for God *and* enthusiastic, even while her heart was breaking: "I gave God my whole life. *The whole thing.* He's telling me that this isn't the spouse He has for me. Being with the wrong mate could interrupt the work He has for me down the road, and I can't risk that. There's just nothing more to say on the matter." She understood that her entire duration on this planet is owned by the Almighty, not just her "ministry" segment (true enthusiasm). Out of that knowledge, and driven by her love for her Master, she willingly took and suffered that loss (passion).

"I'm So Excited"

At its origin, the word "excited" is not about the euphoric feelings that many perceive it to be; rather, it pertains to instigating a desired response. Its components include prompting urges, stirring up emotions, disturbing or agitating, and even "magnetically or electrically...[stimulating]."[64] The irony about this word is that it is probably used most often by people who assume that being excited is a positive thing. But that's not always true. The outcome or direction of the word completely depends on the prompting involved.

Here's an example. As a hobby, Allie makes lye soap. During the progression, the ingredients must undergo a chemical process wherein a caustic substance is added to a lard and oil blend at a specific temperature. This mixture is then agitated by a hand blender for a certain period of time, after which the liquid begins to solidify and can be poured into molds. After a few days of curing, the substance reaches a solid state, and that's when she can hand out pieces of it to friends and family. By agitating this mixture with heat, whipping, and forgetting about it, she has an end product that can be used; she provokes a response from the ingredients through stimulation. You might say that she "excites" a bucket of lard to become something that can serve a purpose. However, to say that this is a euphoric experience is incorrect. When we say we're excited about what God is doing in our lives, it is vital that we realize this word points to an outcome, not an emotion. We must remember our commitment to that excitement when the transformation begins to push us out of our comfort zone and into something He can use.

God Built His Kingdom for Misfits

We can see a strange dichotomy amongst those who believe Scripture to be true, but still somehow feel they cannot be used by God. It is observed through the notion that we readily believe God used imperfect people in ancient history, but we are somehow exempt from Him using us. If, as we read throughout Scripture, the Lord used outcasts and oddballs for His eternal glory despite the biblical characters' innumerable human failures, then why do Christians today struggle with feeling we can be used the same way? Why do so many appear to respond to the calling on our lives with, "Surely, you're not calling *me*, Lord… You must be looking for my brother, Aaron, right?" What's the hang-up?

We can offer many pessimistic (but sadly accurate) reasons for this problem, from laziness to apathy to the fact that many Christians can't seem to hear the voice of the Holy Spirit above the staticky din of our busy lives. However, for others, there's an almost unexplainable disconnect between today's believers and the imperfect people He called in Scripture. If He could use *them*, why wouldn't He bring about unbelievable miracles through *us*? What's stopping us from jumping into action and watching as mountainous movements of God heal our land and erupt in revivals and Great Awakenings?

Theories abound.

One is worth mentioning here.

The Over-Perfecting of the Saints

Ever heard of a "hagiography"? As fancy as the term sounds, it's easy to understand. It's simply a biography of the saints in extrabiblical history—i.e., what happened in the lives of the men and women of the New Testament (or important leaders of the early church). These texts often cover the saints' past, additional details surrounding their response to the call into ministry, miracles or major events during their peak years that the Bible doesn't record, and, frequently, their eventual martyrdom.

At times, the evidence backing up these stories is sizeable enough to take a little more seriously than others. One example that Donna brought up in her previous work, *The Handmaidens Conspiracy*, was of the woman at the well from John 4. According to the woman's biographers, after the face-to-face with Jesus that changed her forever, this Samaritan woman was baptized by the apostles and renamed Photini ("light" or "enlightened one"). Following His ascension, Jesus came to her in a dream and inspired her to boldly head straight for Rome, wherein she proceeded to witness Christ to Emperor Nero, in person, regardless of any threat of death. Nero, angered by such an act and unable to intimidate her, ordered that Photini (and those with her) be tortured. For hours, unthinkable acts of torment were attempted against Photini and her cohorts, but to no avail. (For instance, when Nero ordered their hands to be smashed with iron rods for an hour, Photini calmly sat quoting from the Psalms, and nobody in her group could be injured, no matter how hard Nero's men tried.) Afterward, Photini refused to denounce Christ in exchange for unthinkable wealth and treasures that would have been bestowed upon her and her company by Nero's daughter, Domnina. Instead, Domnina's offering of riches provided the opportunity for Photini's assembly to witness, and Domnina accepted Christ as her Savior and was baptized on the spot, along with a hundred or so of her palace servants and a sorceress who had been brought in to poison Photini.

Nero, enraged at the news of his daughter's conversion, ordered Photini and her people to be burned alive, but they could not be harmed. Nor did any injury befall them when they were subsequently lined up and forced to drink poison in the presence of the emperor. Nero, in desperation and running out of ideas, threw the lot of them into prison to rot, never thinking that Photini would then proceed to convert all the prison guards and scores of Romans who, out of mere curiosity, went to visit this woman whom Nero could not kill.

This "other side to the story" regarding the Samaritan woman is documented in Eastern Orthodox tradition, the writings of the church fathers, historians and biographers of the Byzantine era, and ancient Greek sermons from the fourth to the fourteenth century. Because of the span of years and number of people/witnesses from varying geographical regions who all claimed these events were true, there may actually be some (or a lot of) truth behind this story. On the other hand, since it's extrabiblical, we cannot know for sure that any of it is, and no believers should put all of their faith in God into something outside the Word. On the other other hand, no texts hold the same authority as Scripture, yet many historical documents (including biographies) are true. (It cracks these authors up when believers get nervous about reading extrabiblical, noncanonical texts regarding biblical events or characters on the grounds that they aren't in the Bible and are therefore automatically suspect, but these same folks will pick up a biography of Albert Einstein—also extrabiblical information—and not even think to question whether Einstein's biographer was romanticizing a portion of *his* life. If people can bring themselves to believe the miracles of the Bible, there is nothing shocking about the idea that Jesus inspired a radical female minister who lived to see miracles similar to what occurred around the apostles in the New Testament.) Either way, true or false, this story of "Saint Photini" is what is known as a "hagiography."

Granted, many (though not all) of these documents are suspect anyway, as they're sometimes traced to biased recordkeeping of the earlier

Roman Catholic Church, whose political and social agenda at the time was power and domination, and therefore mass manipulation. Hagiographies assisted religious leaders in this goal, and it kind of makes sense, even though it's tragic deceit at its worst. The hagiography of an early-church saint who was flawlessly pious, morally perfect, great in charity, and less in pride (and so on and so forth, flowery words) could climax in some grand act that would then be championed by the Roman Church in support of whatever scheme it was brewing that season. Consider it the influential "fake news" memes of the early church leading up to the Protestant Reformation. For instance: If an early pope wanted to sell indulgences (these, literally, are monies given to papal leadership in exchange for the absolving of sin and lesser punishment in the purgatorial afterlife), he would never find support for such an evil thing in the Bible unless he was willing to twist Scripture (which some did). However, he could easily make up the words or actions of a saint from a totally fake biography to set an example about the sales of indulgences and sway the masses with a sort of, "If the holy Saint Peter did [fill in the blank], then it *must* be fine" stance. (Additionally, many events described in the hagiographies of other saints aren't verifiable in any historical texts outside the hagiography itself, which casts doubt on the credibility of the story.)

But aside from suspicious origins, papal manipulations, and lack of proof, unfortunately, the hagiographical accounts of the saints are often perceived as the fabricated imaginings of a poorhouse scribe, because they tend to paint pictures of unrealistically perfect people: men and women who are spotless to the point that they defy the fallen nature that's plagued every human since Adam and Eve.

Today, we can see through a lot of these overly romanticized retellings, but it should be noted that the Roman Catholic Church's influence on "the pure and perfect saints of Christ" through fraudulent hagiographies did eventually contribute to a twofold (and confusing) corporate concept within the Church Body: God *does* use regular people to accomplish His work…but just, uhhh, not *you*, because you're not as impressive as [insert name of saint here], whose hagiography shows him to be much holier and more pious than you in his everyday life. The dichotomy of the "perfect saint" on one hand with the "average Joe God will use" on the other has always been incompatible. However, it has been accepted just enough to solidify a communally shared (though never declared), anomalous, oxymoronic theology: God is all-powerful, so anyone *can* be used…but only the special ones *will* be.

In a nutshell, those who've gone before are exalted to be remembered only for their good deeds—and that's if all the stories we hear are true in the first place. Any mistakes they may have made over the course of their lives are either whitewashed away or become the pinnacle event by which the rest of their lives are launched into tales of religious success—which, in its own way, likewise memorializes any human blunders under the always-justified header of "yeah, this guy *totally* blew it! But it's good, because look how God used him next!" In hindsight, we are able to see God's redemption. The deed has been forgiven and its aftermath used for the good of God's plan for the individual's life, so the act of sin itself is diminished. Yet, as human beings traversing the course of time, we're not afforded such a perspective during our own lives. We are experiencing this in real time—*not* as rendered by a historical media printed a hundred years after our deaths, when our own mistakes would be diminished and weighed against the positive influence of our own lives. It's often said that an artist is not appreciated until he or she passes away. The same is true of the glorification of these people who once walked the earth just like all of us flawed human beings who are seeking to navigate the awkward, painful, and challenging course of life.

Donna was talking one day with her husband about the crafty art of hagiography and how it has shaped people's view of lofty religious characters when he said, "The Roman Catholics introduced a standard that was unmatchable and even unobtainable. So, today's saints are misled to believe that we shouldn't even try. What chance do we [who see the world in real-time, as I just explained] have to be like those saints? These records *must be* describing somebody else."

For some bizarre and unexplainable reason, we occasionally hear someone say they find the Bible hard to believe because the characters within it are such a mess. From Adam forward, just about every key person in the Word, at one point or another, knowingly participates in some horrible act of sin against God, which often also inflicts pain or calamity on those around the offender. These men and women of the Bible are frequently the opposite of good behavioral examples. The Bible is supposed to be a moral compass, but its central characters—whose lives and decisions we're expected to learn from—can't even conform to its holiness standards. How can the "Word of God," the very revelation of God's perfect nature and will to humankind, be told through a bunch of reckless sinners?

Skywatch broadcaster Derek Gilbert's favorite response to this question is: "Anything less would present a historical record of human nature that could never be believed. Actually, it argues for the authenticity of the Bible that many of its central characters are part-time reprobates."

However, at the end of the day, there is no denying that our Lord chose *regular, human* people with regular, human problems and weaknesses to accomplish great things for His Kingdom.

God picked the misfits, the outcasts, the awkward, and even the most sinful to become those whose lives were transformed to holiness and eventually memorialized in Scripture precisely *because* they would seem the least likely for such ambitions. It is in their flawed humanity that these people are relatable and even familiar.

Many of us have personalities that can be compared directly to one of these biblical examples that are now elevated in such realms as our churches or Bible studies as great examples of God's power working through everyday people. We identify their character traits in ourselves—how we make decisions, what passions we have, our ability to doubt or to have faith, and how we respond to something that touches our heart.

Consider even the twelve misfits Jesus surrounded Himself with during His days on earth. We struggle just as they sometimes did, yet they were the ones who lived in close proximity to Him, witnessed His death and resurrection, and received the Great Commission from Him (Matthew 28:19). Most of them were eventually martyred after launching the most revolutionary and world-changing religion the world has ever seen. Perhaps we face overwhelming odds in life and, in that moment, feel a touch of Peter-like fear such as that he manifested on the night of Christ's arrest that contributed to his denial of the precious Messiah (Matthew 26:33–35; Mark 14:29–31; Luke 22:33–34; John 18:15–27). Maybe when we experience rejection, we, too, throw out a knee-jerk reaction similar to the time when James and John asked Jesus if they should call fire down from heaven to consume a town that didn't show them hospitality (Luke 9:54). Or, possibly, we have "pulled a Thomas" once or twice in the past when the Bible doesn't align with our expectations and we, too, demand satisfying proof from God before we can accept what testimony He has provided through His Word (John 20:25). Each of these had to make a conscious decision to set their humanity aside and plow straight into what they've been called to do for the Messiah; the result was the eventual launch and growth of the largest religion in the world—all for the most part stemming from the tenacity of twelve regular guys.

Although some readers might know the basics regarding the Twelve, others might be newer to the subject, so we'll include this as a friendly reminder here… Ahem…

The disciples were not theologians!

Jesus didn't have "a type" when He called these men. They spanned a wide variety of social classes and societal credentials as well; they were everything from tax collectors to zealots to fishermen to tradesmen to craftsmen and all in between. Jesus absolutely could have chosen to empower from on high twelve rabbis, or even some more powerful names from the Sanhedrin. Don't think it isn't possible—and we shouldn't kid ourselves for a moment by thinking that this fact isn't enormously important. The interest that the Sanhedrin's own Nicodemus and Joseph of Arimathea took in Jesus shows that Christ could have easily handpicked wealthy, respectable theologians of His day to represent Him and inaugurate the fledgling Church. The fact that He didn't is crucial. God, Himself, in the flesh, specifically sought out and called those who were *not* scholars, theologians, rabbis, or scribes. As one biblical commentator puts it: "The propagation of the gospel and the founding of the church hinged entirely on twelve men whose most outstanding characteristic was their ordinariness."[65] The same scholar points out a page or two later that, within the three years' ministry of Christ—with the disciples' calling having taken place almost exactly at the midway point—the Twelve received *less than half* the training time under Christ than it would take to earn a modern seminary degree before they were released on their own to spread the Good News to the ends of the earth.

There appears to be an attitude of exclusion in today's world against anyone who wants to join a discussion on biblical topics but who doesn't have seminary degrees behind his or her name. (And if the person *is* a "her," the oppressive spirit becomes twice as hard to fight against in many religious circles where Scripture is still erroneously being interpreted to oppose women teachers, preachers, pastors, etc. Donna deals at length with this issue in her book, *Handmaidens Conspiracy*.) We see this online a lot: Someone posts a YouTube video about a Bible verse (or something similar), and online trolls are quick to question why the poster is qualified to say a word when their expertise is in another field. And while all true disciples of Christ should careful what we say about the Lord's Word (the responsibility we take to know the Word before we speak about it is a heavy burden, indeed!), the opposite approach—that one must be officially trained to be effective—is unnecessarily limiting, and the Bible is filled with the stories of men and women as proof.

It's crucial that we make this point: *Every Christian has been called into ministry or service of some type.* If you've been doubting this, then pretty please with a cherry on top wipe all of that from your thoughts and start over by looking at who was present at the *true* beginning: the Almighty, All-Powerful Ruler over every force in the cosmos. *And*, He made a personal appearance to offer salvation and empower His followers here on earth.

Followers like us. Regular, everyday people. Do you get our drift yet? The Church Jesus came to build is made up of average, flawed, non-seminary-attending, non-theologian folks whose lives were as imperfect as ours.

That following started as a dozen average men. That's it. Jesus Himself was a rabbi, so He was personally viewed as an expert on the Scriptures, but the Twelve were not. Nor, by the way, were they masterful orators. They weren't trained philosophers, and none of them held any special education in the art of challenge and riposte so expected from the great Greek-cultured minds of that day. Even Jesus personally acknowledged that His disciples were less familiar with the Scripture than they should have been, and that deficit impacted how "slow" they were at recognizing what the prophets of old had said would be regarding His death and suffering (Luke 24:25–27). Let this stand as a shining example as to why you, yourself—whether you be male, female, boss, or employee (cf. Galatians 3:28)—*do not* have to be an expert on the Bible or have any background in the art of speech in order to be used mightily of God in the area of your calling.

You could be like any one of the disciples who, ordinary as they may have been, "turned the world upside down" for the sake of the gospel (Acts 17:6).

Cornelius: The Roman-Centurion-Orphan-Misfit Who Changed Church-Growth History

Throughout this work, we've discussed Yukon Cornelius, the strange, pick-axe-licking character in the 1964 *Rudolph* movie who, as it happens, was seeking a peppermint mine for the duration of the film. However, Donna would like to turn back the clock a bit and spend some time talking about a different Cornelius: one spoken of in the book of Acts. Here, in her own words, is what she discovered, and the account of how she discovered it:

I recently conducted a one-question survey with some friends and a few folks from my inner circle here at SkyWatch and Defender Publishing for a school project. It was an easy question:

What is a "Gentile"?

I asked all participants—a group that included laymen as well as biblical scholars—for a brief, simple response. Here are the answers I got:

- "A Gentile is a non-Jew," one said.
- "A non-Jew," said another.
- "Hmm. A *short* answer?" replied one scholarly friend. (I anticipated being there a while, but he was gracious.) "I'd have to say 'non-Jew.'"
- Thomas Horn said, "A non-Jew in the first century."
- James Howell, my husband, said, "Without thinking about it? It's a non-Jew."
- One of my favorites, from an intelligent Christian friend who fancies herself a comedian: "Ain't that a dude who ain't a Jew?"
- Hilariously, Allie Henson, responding by a quickly read text, said, "Fast answer? It means more feminine than masculine but not about gender. Somewhat demure, 'genteel' is a demeanor more than a behavior. [Five minutes later…] Oh '*Gentile*'! LOL! That changes everything! My *initial* thought would be to say 'a non-Jew,' but in another project I would probably elaborate and say it was tied into one's submission to Old Testament laws."

By now, the collective response among the men and women I surveyed, who are well-versed in the Word, is that a "Gentile" was a person in the first century who wasn't a Jew. With that in the bag, I went off to work and filled my head with other thoughts.

That night, back at my home office, I was in deep study of the book of Acts. One verse distracted me in a way that it hadn't before. It stated, as a *fact* (not as a matter of opinion or something that could be "interpreted away"), that Cornelius, a Roman centurion of the Italian Regiment, was "a devout man...who feared God" (Acts 10:2; NKJV).

I blinked. It popped out at me so I read it again: "devout man...who feared God." *Our* God, the God of the Bible.

Of course, I had read this verse before, many times. And I knew that there *was* a certain oddball group of non-Jews who, at least in part, followed the Jewish God but were not wholly proselytes (Gentiles who converted to Judaism). This group was referred to by the loose term "God-fearers," and they were attracted to the God of the Jews because of His high ethical/moral standard and purity. My college textbook expounds:

> At that time in human history only Judaism taught monotheism; all other religions had multitudes of gods and goddesses. Only Judaism had high ethical standards. In the other religions, gods would [abuse] goddesses, and new gods and goddesses would be born. Prostitution was a liturgical part of religious worship. At that time, half the world was enslaved. Only Judaism promised a coming Messiah or Deliverer. Many Gentiles were attracted to the Jewish concepts of monotheism, high ethical standards, and a promised Messiah-Deliverer.[66]

These Gentiles were the "God-fearers." Most scholars agree that "God fearers" isn't a technical term.[67,68] But while they may slightly differ from your average "Gentile," they are still considered Gentiles:

> It is likely, at least for Gentile men, that the prospect of circumcision was one of the reasons some "God fearers" never became

full coverts. Other reasons, such as social or ethnic concerns could also have been factors. "God fearers," whatever their connection and affection for Judaism, *remained fully Gentile.* (Emphasis added)[69]

But an association with the word "Gentile" that carries some unfortunate baggage as well. Yes, "Gentile" primarily means "non-Jew," and that identifies a nationality—i.e., someone who isn't born into Jewish blood. In this sense, I have no problem using the term for Cornelius or anyone else. It would hardly be any different from identifying people as "non-African" if they were born Chinese.

However, and this is crucial: The word "Gentile" in Greek (*ethnikos*) and Hebrew (*goy*) is used in many places throughout the Bible, in both the Old *and* New Testaments, as a reference to "heathens" or "pagans" (see Deuteronomy 18:9; Galatians 2:15; Ephesians 2:12; and many others). In *The Lexham Bible Dictionary*, under a section titled "Jewish Attitudes Towards Gentiles," we read that one definition of the word at that time was: "Unrighteous—a stereotype of Gentiles as examples of unrighteous behavior...with no hope for salvation (Eph 2:12; *Jubilees* 15:26)."[70] Another Bible dictionary explains: "In course of time, as the Jews began more and more to pride themselves on their peculiar privileges, [the word 'Gentile'] acquired unpleasant associations, and was *used as a term of contempt*" (emphasis added).[71] Dang...that's a strong feeling. Look, too, at how Jesus, Himself, uses this term in Matthew 18:17: "but if he neglect to hear the church, let him be unto thee as an heathen man [*ethnikos*, "Gentile"] and a publican." For good reason, many Bible translations read "let him be to you as a Gentile or tax collector."

Yet, most scholars acknowledge that "Cornelius believed in the God of the Jews and was committed to honoring him from a sincere and submissive heart."[72]

It wasn't new to me that the God of the Jews was the same God Cornelius devotedly followed, and I knew that the "happy ending" was mere verses away, when Peter would be summoned from Joppa and lead Cornelius and his entire household to Christ…but it was *this* verse, in *this* very moment in time, *before* Cornelius accepted the Messiah, that I couldn't let go, because suddenly I realized that it was God's Word identifying "devout man…who feared God." There was a lesson hidden here in plain sight that was being missed by too many Bible readers, including myself, up to this moment. After the "Gentile" survey, something was no longer settling well. What started as just a tiny hiccup in my own comprehension that I chose to ignore continued to nag at the back of my mind until I relented and gave it my whole focus.

I glanced back to my survey notes defining "Gentile": "not a Jew, not a Jew, not a Jew…"

I glanced back to the Acts 10:2 description of Cornelius: "a devout man…who feared [the Jewish] God."

"What *are* you?" I said aloud, shaking my head.

Sure, I knew Cornelius would have been called a "Gentile" at the time. He wasn't even circumcised. But, deep down, I saw with fresh perspective that there was a title game being played around that turn in history…and something about it felt too familiar.

A fledgling thought was whipping about in my mind and I decided to act on it. I backed my chair away from my study table, grabbed my phone, and headed to my computer to send some texts and emails to my inner circle again. I sent out another one-question survey and asked the participants to keep their answers as concise as possible, just like the first time.

What is a "Jew"?

I asked everyone to approach the question as if it was being asked around the first century, close to the time of the cross, to try to put us in the same headspace as those characters in Acts. Additionally, I made it clear that this was not a racial or national question that had anything to do with whether a person had been *born* into a Jewish tribe or family, etc. When I asked what a "Jew" was, I was asking about a spiritual identity.

Most of the answers were exactly what I expected to hear:

- "A follower of Yahweh."
- "Someone who followed God before Christ."
- "A participant in the pre-Christian religion of the Old Testament."
- "A person who made Jehovah their God."

Again, I looked at the verse in Acts 10:2, thinking maybe I missed something.

Poor Cornelius, I thought to myself. *You aren't circumcised, you probably don't observe all the feasts, you likely don't follow all the rules, and as such, you would probably be ostracized from, or at least cold-shouldered at, any a synagogue where you tried to sincerely worship... But you're devoted to the same God as the Jews! Spiritually, you are a Jew or proselyte! Yet you are doomed to fail in your pursuit to fit into any religious family in those days unless you adhere to a bunch of rote rules.*

Other than circumcision and a few other rituals, what *was* the difference between a "God-fearer" and a legitimate proselyte?

I looked it up in my Logos Bible Software and read that I was not the first to think these terms bore uncanny resemblance, as *Holman Illustrated Bible Dictionary* stated: "One should be careful about drawing too sharp a distinction between 'God fearer' and the technical term 'proselyte.'"[73]

It was now pretty late. Maybe I would figure it all out in the morning. Meanwhile, I was lying in bed, waiting to fall asleep, asking myself why, if he followed their God so dutifully as to be called "devout," Cornelius wouldn't have pursued officially converting. At least *then*, he and his household wouldn't feel like outsiders. Was his stance against circumcision? I mean, he was about to be freed from that as an obligation through the New Covenant anyway, but *he* didn't know that yet...

"One more survey," I texted everyone the first thing the next morning. "Then I promise I'll leave you all alone."

It included the same parameters as the previous two: short answer, first-century application:

How does one become a proselyte?

As you can imagine, this was the part that shifted *away* from deeply spiritual concepts and into ritual. Everyone had the same idea:

- "Get circumcised and start obeying the Mosaic Law."
- "Carry out a burnt animal sacrifice."
- "Observe all the laws and precepts that the Jews had to."
- "Circumcision; sacrifice; baptism ritual; Law."
- And, from my funny friend: "Get a degree in legalism."

As my phone was blowing up with answers from my associates and friends, I left the room to go get a cup of coffee and say hello to my husband. I asked him the proselyte question as well and, after placing him within the boundaries of a "short" answer, he paused, stopped chewing his reheated goulash from dinner the night before, and shrugged, eyes wide, shaking his head.

- "Man... I just don't know. Follow a bunch of *rules*, I guess?"

The distasteful emphasis he placed on the word "rules" made this whole Cornelius thing click. From out of the mouth of the gorgeous, bearded man in my dining room came the answer I hadn't been able to put my finger on during the last few days.

That was the problem. Cornelius was a spiritual orphan.

Cornelius is *not* definable by terms such as "Jew" or "proselyte." That much we've established. He is not a "Christian" (called a "follower of the Way" at the time), because, at this moment in Acts 10:2, he hasn't heard the gospel yet. Nor would "pagan" be accurate, since he, as identified out of the very God-breathed Scripture, is a devoted, God-fearing man...and this is precisely why "Gentile" doesn't sound appropriate either, because it's synonymous with "pagan" and linked to those "with no hope for salvation."[74]

We're back to Cornelius being a spiritual orphan. He's not a Jew, proselyte, Christian, pagan, heathen, or Gentile (spiritually speaking). He's a misfit on a grand scale—an oddball who doesn't have a family or anyone that he can connect to.

Nothing about it was right. If you sat him down to talk theology with a Jew from his day, the two would come to realize they were following the SAME GOD; they would have the same essential beliefs! He is, according to our verse study, referred to with the same adjective ("devout") that identified some of the grandest of biblical heroes who did enormous, miraculous works in the name of Yahweh/Christ. But because he didn't jump through the *legal* hoops, he was an orphan. A Jew of his day might have been willing to witness to him about his religion, but the second Cornelius had a different idea about the rules, the rituals, the laws, the sacrifices…a Pharisee would have written him off. Jesus saw this problem, and had a dramatic answer: "Woe unto you, scribes and Pharisees, hypocrites! For ye compass sea and land to make one proselyte, and when he is made, ye make him twofold more the child of hell than yourselves" (Matthew 23:15).

Poor orphan Cornelius.

How many Corneliuses do you think are in My Body today, but have no family because the hoops of modern, religious legalism have ostracized them, as well? I heard that Still, Small Voice ask me.

"Many," I fumed, shaking my head and feeling that old familiar "Rise Up, Radicals!" sermon starting to bubble up in my heart again. "Lord," I prayed, taking a deep breath. "What do you want me to do?"

When you meet a Cornelius, remind him or her that it is MY definition that matters—not the word games humans play.

My eyes fell back to Acts 10:2, and I blinked back tears. Right there, as I had always known but never fully grasped, was God, Himself, in His own Words, identifying, defining, refining, and now redefining Cornelius the way God always saw him: "a devout man...who feared God." No other word, term, title, label, tagline, stamp, mark, or even nickname mattered anymore, and never would again. Cornelius' *heart* was in the right place, and that is what God had always observed.

Oh...and before I go, let me tell you the poetic relevance of Cornelius' Acts 10–11 happy ending:

An angel came to Cornelius and instructed him to call for Peter in Joppa. In a divine appointment, just before Cornelius' men arrived over in Joppa to summon Peter, Peter had a vision of his own, the interpretation of which illustrated that Gentiles can be equal inheritors of salvation (Acts 10:9–15, 28). The very *next* event recorded in Scripture was this: Peter went willingly with Cornelius' men and proceeded to witness the gospel to the "many" who were gathered in the home of Cornelius (Acts 10:27). Before he had finished, the Holy Spirit fell upon the entire assembly and, to the amazement of the Jewish Christians, they all spoke in tongues (Acts 10:44–48), which marked the inauguration of the Gentiles into the church, and into the family of God.

Know what that means? Consider it on a larger scale: *Now* the gospel would be recognized as extending not only to believing Jews, but to *every single person in the world from that moment forward.* Although the crowd, as it is physically and literally accounted for on this precise day, is only Cornelius and his household (which included family, friends, and servants), it *launched* the largest church-growth contributor in human history. In this instance, we're not only considering an increase in its numbers, but it involves a spiritual growth also, as that group of believers matured into a new diverse family and took on a new attitude of acceptance. The previously generic "God-fearers" became *paramount* to the advancement of the early church!

In Acts the "God fearers" are key figures in the unfolding of God's plan of redemption.... Furthermore, as the gospel spread to Pisidian Antioch, to Philippi, to Corinth, to Athens, and beyond, the "God fearers" were among those who formed the earliest Christian congregations as the gospel spread to the Gentiles.[75]

And it all started with Cornelius, who proved that it is *only* through fearing God, following Him, and carrying out righteous deeds that we are found acceptable to God (Acts 10:35), not through titles and word games.

Thank you for your diligence, Mr. Misfit Without A Spiritual Family. Thank you for your service to God when nobody was looking, Mr. Nobody Knows What To Call You. Thank you for standing as a powerful challenger of legalism, Mr. Non-Jew In The Presence Of Our Jewish Savior.

Thank you, misfits, oddballs, and outcasts everywhere.

The orphan, through diligently following God with the sincerity of his heart, paved the way for the spiritual adoption of every other orphan, forever.

Including *me*, a non-Jew of the twenty-first century.

Are You Ready?

In closing this work, we authors ask you once more: Are you inspired? Enthusiastic? Excited? Impassioned? Are you owned by God and sold out to His purpose, ready and empowered to see it through, even when it stretches you, pulls you from your comfort zone, or requires you to make sacrifices for His service? Are you ready to drop the self-limiting and segregating narrative that says you are unqualified or not good enough?

Are you ready to subscribe to all God has for your life, to see yourself through His loving eyes, to see the *unique, individually specific* potential in yourself rather than the awkward, ineligible or incapable misfit you've previously chosen to see? Are you finally prepared to step out from hiding—off the Island of Misfits—and into a beautiful world of one-of-a-kind people with whom you blend beautifully because you, too, are completely matchless?

There is work to be done, and you're part of it. You belong here. Your skills, talents, interests, perspectives, personality, and even your failures matter here. The family of God—which is made up completely of adopted spiritual orphans—is waiting for you to join us. No perfection required! The Kingdom of God has been built and will continue to be built using rag-tag, eccentric oddballs just like us, and just like you. If your status as an exile has caused you to sequester in a remote place without the fellowship of others, it is time to come home—to find your unparalleled place in this beautiful, mixed-up, flawed-but-forgiven bunch called the Body of Christ.

Notes

1. *The Greatest Showman*, starring Hugh Jackman, written by Jenny Bicks and Bill Condon, directed by Michael Gracey, produced by Peter Churnin et al, released December 20, 2017, 21:36–22:17.
2. Ibid., 22:41–22:48.
3. Ibid., 22:48–23:37.
4. Ibid., 23:22–23:27.
5. Ibid., 26:22–27:22.
6. Ibid., 56:59–57:35.
7. May, Robert L. *Rudolph the Red-Nosed Reindeer: Plus "Rudolph Shines Again."* AudioGO. Kindle Edition, location 6.
8. May, Robert L. "Rudolph Created in a Time of Sadness," as quoted by: Nate Bloom, "Shining a Light on the Largely Untold Story of the Origins of Rudolph, the Red-Nosed Reindeer," December 20, 2011, *InterFaithFamily*, last accessed July 19, 2019, https://www. interfaithfamily.com/arts_and_entertainment/popular_culture/ Shining_a_Light_on_the_Largely_Untold_Story_of_the_ Origins_of_Rudolph_the_Red-Nosed_Reindeer/.
9. Ibid.

10. Goldschmidt, Rick. *The Making of the Rankin/Bass Holiday Classic: Rudolph the Red-Nosed Reindeer* (Miser Bros Press, Kindle Edition), location 112.

11. Ibid., locations 1247–1255.

12. *Rudolph the Red-Nosed Reindeer*, written by Romeo Muller, directed by Larry Roemer and Kizo Nagashima, narrated by Burl Ives, composed by Johnny Marks, produced by Arthur Rankin Jr. and Jules Bass, originally aired December 6th, 1964 on NBC Television's *The General Electric Fantasy Hour*, 4:36–5:19.

13. Ibid., 6:20–7:00.

14. Ibid., 9:48–10:13.

15. Ibid., 11:40–13:36.

16. Ibid., 17:17–18:38.

17. Cole, R. A., *Exodus: An Introduction and Commentary: Volume 2* (Downers Grove, IL: InterVarsity Press; 1973), 60.

18. Jamieson, R., Fausset, A. R., & Brown, D., *Commentary Critical and Explanatory on the Whole Bible: Volume 1* (Oak Harbor, WA: Logos Research Systems, Inc.; 1997), 48.

19. Rawlinson, George, *Ellicott's Commentary for English Readers*, "Exodus 1," last accessed on *BibleHub* July 12, 2021, https:// biblehub.com/commentaries/ellicott/exodus/1.htm.

20. Dr. Eisenberg, R. L. *The JPS Guide to Jewish Traditions* (Philadelphia: The Jewish Publication Society; 1st ed., 2004), 14.

21. Cole, R. A., *Exodus*, 64.

22. Jamieson, R., Fausset, A. R., & Brown, D., *Commentary*, 48.

23. Cole, R. A., *Exodus*, 63–64; emphasis added.

24. Ibid.

25. Jamieson, R., Fausset, A. R., & Brown, D., *Commentary*, 49.

26. Ross, A., & Oswalt, J. N., *Cornerstone Biblical Commentary: Genesis, Exodus: Volume 1* (Carol Stream, IL: Tyndale House Publishers; 2008), 293.

27. Barnes, Albert, *Barnes Notes on the Whole Bible* (E4 Group, Kindle Edition), Kindle locations 229914–229918).

28. Jamieson, R., Fausset, A. R., & Brown, D., *Commentary*, 180; emphasis added.

29. Heiser, Dr. Michael, "Exodus 4:1–17," March 23, 2019, *Naked Bible Podcast*, transcript of episode 264, last accessed July 15, 2021, quoted material from page 8: https://nakedbiblepodcast. com/wp-content/uploads/2019/03/NB-264-Transcript.pdf.

30. Barnes, Albert, *Barnes*, Kindle locations 9494–9495.

31. Jamieson, R., Fausset, A. R., & Brown, D., *Commentary*, 282.

32. Cole, R. A., *Exodus*, 66.

33. Barnes, Albert, *Barnes*, Kindle locations 9497–9498.

34. Poole, Matthew, *Matthew Poole's Commentary*, "Exodus 2," last accessed on *BibleHub* July 20, 2021, https://biblehub.com/ commentaries/poole/exodus/2.htm.

35. Ibid.

36. Ibid.

37. Gill, John, *Gill's Exposition*, "Exodus 2," last accessed on *BibleHub* July 20, 2021, https://biblehub.com/commentaries/gill/ exodus/2.htm.

38. Brooks, R., "Mishnah." In D. N. Freedman (Ed.), *The Anchor Yale Bible Dictionary: Volume 4* (New York: Doubleday; 1992), 871.

39. Eisenberg, R. L., *The JPS Guide to Jewish Traditions* (1st ed.; Philadelphia: The Jewish Publication Society; 2004), 637.

40. Brown, F., Driver, S. R., & Briggs, C. A., *Enhanced Brown-Driver-Briggs Hebrew and English Lexicon* (Oxford: Clarendon Press; 1977), 922.

41. Though this order can't be proven, if these authors are wrong in our breakdown of what happened, how it happened, and when it happened in this fuzzy, Hebrews-versus-Exodus section on Moses' life, then so are a collection of about fifty authors/

scholars/theologians whose books and writings were consulted before we made these estimates. Rather than to create a lengthy and distracting list of citations here, which would involve at least another "chapter's length" of what we found and where, who compared to who in the academic world, how denominational interpretations differed and led us to other conclusions and so on, the readers are encouraged to look back on all the citations we have provided in this area. These are all readily available, free online, and—*though they often to not specifically state the conclusion we made about the night of Moses' murder being the same night he took on the posture of Hebrews 11:24–26*—the collectively come to nearly identical conclusions once the whole of their writings on Moses are considered.

42. Jamieson, R., Fausset, A. R., & Brown, D., *Commentary*, 50.

43. Ibid.

44. Ibid.

45. Rankin, Arthur, producer. *Rudolph the Red-Nosed Reindeer.* Rankin/Bass Productions, 1964. DVD, 47 min.

46. Gallups, Carl. *Masquerade: Prepare for the Greatest Con Job in History.* 2020. Crane, MO: Defender Publishing, LLC. P. 109.

47. Dodson, Bob. "The Request For the Inheritance:Part 1 of the Study of the Lost Son Parable in Luke 15." Acts 242 Study. Last Accessed July 26, 2021. https://acts242study.com/the-request-for-the-inheritance-part-1-of-the-study-of-the-lost-son-parable-in-luke-15/.

48. Ibid.

49. Ibid.

50. Ibid.

51. *Rudolph the Red-Nosed Reindeer*, written by Romeo Muller, directed by Larry Roemer and Kizo Nagashima, narrated by Burl Ives, composed by Johnny Marks, produced by Arthur Rankin

Jr. and Jules Bass, originally aired December 6th, 1964 on NBC Television's *The General Electric Fantasy Hour*, 4:36–5:19.

52. Horn, Joe. *Everyday Champions: Unleash the Gifts God Gave You, Step into Your Purpose, and Fulfil Your Destiny.* (2019). Crane, MO: Defender Publishing, LLC. P. 92-93.

53. Batistelli, Francesca. "If We're Honest." (2014) *If We're Honest.* (Album). Nashville, TN: Word Records.

54. Sullivan, Kevin. Producer/Director. *Anne of Green Gables.* Toronto, Canada: Sullivan Entertainment. 1985. DVD, 195 min.

55. Strong's H2896, *Blue Letter Bible Online*, last accessed July 26, 2021, https://www.blueletterbible.org/lexicon/h2896/kjv/wlc/0-1/.

56. Murphy, Jack, lyrics. Wildhorn, Frank, composer. As recorded by Linda Eder, vocalist. *Gold.* New York, NY: Right Track Studios. 2002.

57. Smith, William. *A complete Etymology of the English Language.* 1867. New York, Cincinnati, Chigago: American Book Company, p. 52.

58. Ayto, John. *Dictionary of Word Origins.* 1990. New York, NY: Arcade Publishing, p. 494.

59. "Inspire." Onions, C.T., editor. *The Oxford Dictionary of English Etymology.* Oxford, Great Britain: University Press, p. 477.

60. Strong's H5301, *Blue Letter Bible Online*, last accessed July 26, 2021, https://www.blueletterbible.org/lexicon/h5301/kjv/wlc/0-1/.

61. "Passion." Onions, C.T., editor. *The Oxford Dictionary of English Etymology.* Oxford, Great Britain: University Press, p. 656.

62. Barnhart, Robert, editor. *The Barnhart Concise Dictionary of Etymology.* 1995. New York, NY: Harper Collins Publishers, p. 245.

63. "Enthusiasm." *Chambers Dictionary of Etymology.* New York, NY: Chambers Harrap Publishers, LTD, p. 333.

64. "Excite." *Chambers Dictionary of Etymology*. New York, NY: Chambers Harrap Publishers, LTD, p. 352.

65. MacArthur, J. F., Jr., *Twelve Ordinary Men: How the Master Shaped His Disciples for Greatness, and What He Wants to Do with You* (Nashville, TN: W Publishing Group [a division of Thomas Nelson]; 2002), xiii.

66. Wood, George. 2004. Acts. 3rd ed. Springfield, MO: Global University Press, p.194

67. Vickers, B. J. 2003. "God Fearer." In C. Brand, C. Draper, A. England, S. Bond, E. R. Clendenen, & T. C. Butler (Eds.), Holman Illustrated Bible Dictionary. Nashville, TN: Holman Bible Publishers. p. 662.

68. Bruce, F. F. 1988. The Book of the Acts. Grand Rapids, MI: Wm. B. Eerdmans Publishing Co, p. 203.

69. Vickers, B. J. 2003. "God Fearer." In C. Brand, C. Draper, A. England, S. Bond, E. R. Clendenen, & T. C. Butler (Eds.), Holman Illustrated Bible Dictionary. Nashville, TN: Holman Bible Publishers. p. 662.

70. Chambers, C. 2016. "Gentiles." In J. D. Barry, D. Bomar, D. R. Brown, R. Klippenstein, D. Mangum, C. Sinclair Wolcott, … W. Widder (Eds.), The Lexham Bible Dictionary. Bellingham, WA: Lexham Press.

71. Easton, M. G. 1893. Illustrated Bible Dictionary and Treasury of Biblical History, Biography, Geography, Doctrine, and Literature. New York: Harper & Brothers, p. 282.

72. Laney, J. C. 2019. "Peter and the Centurion Cornelius (Acts 10:1–48)." In B. J. Beitzel, J. Parks, & D. Mangum (Eds.), Lexham Geographic Commentary on Acts through Revelation. Bellingham, WA: Lexham Press, p. 261.

73. Vickers, B. J. 2003. "God Fearer." In C. Brand, C. Draper, A. England, S. Bond, E. R. Clendenen, & T. C. Butler (Eds.),

Holman Illustrated Bible Dictionary. Nashville, TN: Holman Bible Publishers. p. 662.

74. Chambers, C. 2016. "Gentiles." In J. D. Barry, D. Bomar, D. R. Brown, R. Klippenstein, D. Mangum, C. Sinclair Wolcott, ... W. Widder (Eds.), The Lexham Bible Dictionary. Bellingham, WA: Lexham Press.

75. Vickers, B. J. 2003. "God Fearer." In C. Brand, C. Draper, A. England, S. Bond, E. R. Clendenen, & T. C. Butler (Eds.), Holman Illustrated Bible Dictionary. Nashville, TN: Holman Bible Publishers. p. 662.